Succeeding as a First-Time Parent

HBR WORKING PARENTS SERIES

Tips, stories, and strategies for the job that never ends.

The **HBR Working Parents Series** supports readers as they anticipate challenges, learn how to advocate for themselves more effectively, juggle their impossible schedules, and find fulfillment at home and at work.

From classic issues such as work-life balance and making time for yourself to thorny challenges such as managing an urgent family crisis and the impact of parenting on your career, this series features the practical tips, strategies, and research you need to be—and feel—more effective at home and at work. Whether you're up with a newborn or touring universities with your teen, we've got what you need to make working parenthood work for you.

Books in the series include:

Advice for Working Dads

Advice for Working Moms

Communicate Better with Everyone

Doing It All as a Solo Parent

Getting It All Done

Managing Your Career

Succeeding as a First-Time Parent

Taking Care of Yourself

Two-Career Families

WORKING PARENTS

Tips, stories, and strategies for the job that never ends.

Succeeding as a First-Time Parent

Harvard Business
Review Press
Boston, Massachusetts

Copyright 2022 Harvard Business School Publishing Corporation
All rights reserved
Printed in the United States of America

10 9 8 7 6 5 4 3 2 1

The web addresses referenced in this book were live and correct at the time of the book's publication but may be subject to change.

Cataloging-in-Publication data is forthcoming.

ISBN: 978-1-64782-231-6
eISBN: 978-1-64782-205-7

The paper used in this publication meets the requirements of the American National Standard for Permanence of Paper for Publications and Documents in Libraries and Archives Z39.48-1992.

CONTENTS

Contents

Section 2

The Secret to Your Success
Childcare Essentials for New Working Parents

Section 3

Old Job, New You

Returning to Work After Parental Leave

Contents

Section 4

Do You Need a Time-Out?
*Managing Stress, Exhaustion,
and Overwhelming Emotions*

Section 5

Today Plus 20 Years
Your Career Ahead as a Working Parent

Contents

Epilogue

Find *Your* Success

INTRODUCTION

No Spreadsheet Can Cover This

by Daisy Dowling, Series Editor

By nature, I'm a planner and—I'll admit—a bit of a spreadsheet nerd. So nine years ago, when I found out that I was expecting our first child, I opened up a fresh Excel sheet and got to work. Everything, and I mean *everything*, I thought I needed to do or think through before the baby's arrival made it onto my list—which of course was sortable by date, category, and stakeholder. With so much changing and so much unknown, it gave me a wonderful, reassuring feeling to know that I had ordered the "right" baby bathtub, and that the insurance forms I needed to fill out before leave were already complete, signed, and ready to hand over to HR. A car seat, educational toys, the list of folks my husband should call from the hospital to let them know of our child's arrival? Check, check, and check. And of course I took workplace matters very carefully into account. I already had the corporate backup-care number programmed into my phone, and my parental leave transition plan was one of the longest and most agonizingly detailed PowerPoints I've ever produced.

Was I over engineering things? Absolutely. But I was determined, and doing my best—just as you're determined, and doing your best—to step into parenthood on my front foot, and to do right by my career and family.

Of course, I didn't know what I didn't know. And as I quickly realized, so much of working parenthood will *never* fit in a spreadsheet or be reducible to any PowerPoint slide. Two months after my daughter's birth, I got a dream-job offer that left me scrambling to reconcile my career ambitions and my feelings about being the kind of loving, present parent I wanted to be. Back at work, I knew I would have a new daily schedule and additional logistics to adapt to, but I hadn't realized that I would also have to adapt to a new identity. If I was leaving work at 5:30 p.m. each day to get home to the baby, I worried: *Was I still the hard worker I had always been and still wanted to be?* Communicating wasn't easy: Every time I needed to mention my parenting obligations at the office—like when I had to duck out for a few hours to take my daughter to the pediatrician—I felt like an actor who had forgotten my lines. At home, of course, there were the tense negotiations with my husband, also a first-time working parent, on how to divide up our responsibilities. On top of it all, I needed to figure out how, between the emails and feedings, I could get a good night's sleep.

Here's the kicker: I'm an executive coach. It's my full-time job to help other people push past challenges and obstacles and succeed. But as a rookie working parent, I didn't know where to even start with the challenge of combining career and kids. It was time to admit that my old approaches and tools might not work for me anymore. I needed to think beyond my lists and project plans, and to learn to play a whole new game.

Chances are that your life, career, and ambitions as a working parent look very different from mine. You may be a dad, a single parent by choice, or perhaps you just welcomed twins or a child with complex needs. You may work in a very different field, and you're almost certainly much less Excel-obsessed than I am. But whatever our differences, I'll make a gentle guess that—just like me and every one of the hundreds of working parents I've advised—this first-time working parent thing has thrown you for a bit of a loop, that old tools and approaches may feel limited now, and that you're sailing into uncharted seas. As you do, you'll likely find yourself hovering around a few core questions: *How can I succeed on the job, become the mom or dad I want to be, and remain myself all at the same time? How do I start moving in the right direction?* And, *How can I feel good about how I'm doing along the way?*

This book will help you to tackle those questions, to move toward your own unique, authentic answers—and to feel more confident as you do. The expert voices collected in *Succeeding as a First-Time Parent* offer both perspective and how-to on the big-ticket matters that make the transition to working parenthood so daunting: things like how to find the right childcare, or establish your working parent professional brand, or ramp up your career (if you choose to) post-leave and how to self-coach effectively when you hit dilemmas and setbacks. There's no spreadsheet thinking here: None of these essays will cover which baby bathtub is the right one or how to fill out that benefits form. What this book does focus on is *you*, and helping you navigate into these new waters of career-plus-caregiving safely and with confidence.

My advice on how to use this book: Just read through the table of contents and let it sink in. You'll see that the ideas and advice within are encouraging and no-nonsense. Take a deep breath and begin with a few articles that speak best to your biggest current concerns. Maybe your eye will be immediately drawn to Rebecca Knight's chapter on the return from parental leave. Maybe Marika Lindholm's section on single parenting will be just the kind of advice you've been looking for. Turn to those pages for the real-time support you need. Then, over the weeks to come, repeat.

As you use this book, whether you're waiting for the baby's arrival, planning or returning from leave, or approaching your one-year anniversary of being a working mom or dad, remember: There's no single or Excel-ready model for working parenthood. What worked for your own parents, or your sister, or your friends and colleagues may not work for you. Your own old approaches and tools for getting things done and feeling like a high performer at work may not feel as effective now—and that's OK. Follow your instinct and do what feels right for you, today. Remember, there's no Supreme All-Knowing Working Parent Evaluation Committee passing judgment on your choices or writing up a report card. As long as you're transitioning into working parenthood thoughtfully and intentionally—which is what this book will help you do—then you're doing right by yourself, your career, and your family, all at the same time.

Every Day a New Day

Your Transition to Working Parenthood

Planning Your Maternity or Paternity Leave

by Rebecca Knight

Quick Takes

- Find out how much time you're entitled to
- Draft a transition-out plan and transition-back memo
- Set communication boundaries for your leave
- Let go of work projects while you're away
- Check in with your boss before you return

Taking any amount of time off work can be nerve-wracking, even if it's for a happy event like having or adopting a child. What's the best way to get ready for your parental leave? How should you set boundaries? Should you check in with your team while you're out? And what do you do if you realize that you want to change your work schedule while you're on leave?

What the Experts Say

Very few organizations have "a standard operating procedure" for employees taking parental time off, says Joan C. Williams, founding director of the Center for WorkLife Law at the University of California's Hastings College of the Law. All too often they "Band-Aid together a solution every time someone needs to go on leave," letting the burden fall on the parent-to-be. The lack of parental leave plans in organizations "reflects the disconnect between people's personal lives and their work lives," says Lotte Bailyn, professor, emerita, at the MIT Sloan School of Management. "It should be easier than it is," she says. "The fact is that people have babies; they go on National Guard leave; they get sick; and their parents get sick"—in other words, the need for leave is an inevitable fact of employment. The key is to assume a positive outlook. "It's best if you assume it's going to go well." Here are some pointers.

Get a head start.

You want to start thinking about how you will manage your leave—how much time you will take, whether you'll be in contact, how you will transition back—well in advance. So before you go on leave—ideally before you're even expecting—investigate your organization's policies surrounding how much leave you're entitled to. This information, depending on the size of your organization, is usually available online or in an employee handbook. If you're unsure, contact your HR department. But be mindful about timing. "When you talk to HR depends on your organization's culture," says Bailyn. She says that some people worry that they will be "written off" once they announce their family plans. "Don't wait until the last minute," though. There is a considerable amount of paperwork and contingency planning that needs to happen, and "it takes time for other people to figure out" how to manage your absence, Bailyn says.

Devise a transition strategy.

About a month before your leave, ask your supervisor for help in creating a "transition-out plan," says Williams. This memo "defines everything you do" for the organization, describes where each of your projects stands, and identifies the specific colleagues or temporary workers who will "fill in for you during your leave," she says. Without a plan like this, warns Williams, "your work will be abruptly dumped on others." Bailyn recommends involving your colleagues. "You need to work collectively and creatively to figure out how the work will get done [in your absence]," she says. This should motivate others. "Team members will realize that if and when they need something, the group will support them, too."

Plan your return.

In addition to the transition-out plan, you should create a "transition-back memo" to help set expectations and ensure an "appropriate flow of work for your return," Williams says. "It's very common to come back from leave with either no work or an overwhelming amount of work—both of these are undesirable and a recipe for high attrition." Also think about how you'd like to structure your return to the office. "Be realistic about whether you want to do a gradual return to work" where you start out as part-time and work up to full-time, whether you'd like to negotiate additional work from home days, "or if you'd like to be permanent part-time," she says. Then, depending on your relationship with your boss, explore those possibilities before you go on leave. "If it's going to freak out your manager if you bring this up beforehand, don't," says Williams. "But if your manager is more chill, why not have the information?"

Establish boundaries.

While it's "illegal for a company to ask you to work on your leave," says Williams, "it's practical and considerate to let your colleagues know that you're reachable." She suggests saying something like: *If you need a crucial piece of information from me, here's how to get in touch, and I'll do my best to get back to you as soon as I can.* Just knowing that you're there "if something important comes up will make everyone more comfortable," says Bailyn. And if your leave is longer than three months, you might also consider having regular planned meetings with your team "either in-person or by videoconference" at the three-, four-, and five-month mark, she says. "These meetings are a way to check in with your group and find how everything's going," which will help you when you return.

Identify childcare—ASAP.

Bailyn suggests researching childcare options before your baby is born. Call agencies for recommendations or search online via parent networks. Tour facilities near your home and office. Check references on the places you like best by calling other parents. "High-quality infant day care is difficult to find," she says. If you're hiring a nanny, "secure her at least one month before you return to work," recommends Williams. "It's common for child-care to fall through at the last minute, and it puts your job in jeopardy," she says. Besides, this monthlong over-lap is a good investment for your career and your peace of mind. It allows you to "see your childcare in action," which will help you feel better about leaving your baby. It also helps ensure that your transition back to work is seamless, Williams says.

Let go . . .

Don't be tempted to keep tabs on work projects and office politics while you're away. "You can't say, 'While I am out, I want to be involved in A, B, and C.' You need to let go," says Williams. Failing to do so will likely lead to frustration. "You'll be torn between your very intense new responsibilities and very intense old responsibilities," she says. Involving yourself with work projects while you're on leave is also unfair to the colleagues filling in for you, says Bailyn. "Think about [your leave] as an opportunity to help other people develop," she says. After all, "you should have defined and planned how projects will be dealt with [in your absence]," she says. "Have confidence that your people will handle things the way you would want them to be handled."

. . . and then gear up.

About two weeks before your leave is over, Williams recommends calling your boss to set up a one-hour meeting to review your transition-back plan. "You're not legally obligated to do this—it's a judgment call—but if it were me, I'd do it," she says. The alternative to this preemptive meeting is waiting to discuss your return on your first day back, which increases the likelihood that you will "have either no work or too much work," she says. It's smart to check in with your team too before your official return, says Bailyn.

Be honest with yourself.

This prereturn check-in is also the time when you'll likely make final arrangements about your transition. Remember, though, it's a fluid situation. "You don't know [in advance] how you'll feel physically and emotionally [about going back to work], so you can't make hard-and-fast decisions [ahead of time]," says Bailyn. If you are having second thoughts about going back full-time, think creatively about how you could make the situation work. Bailyn recommends bringing your team in on these discussions. "The problem with flexible arrangements is that they are often individually negotiated and kept in secret," she says. A better option is to work out a proposed plan with your team that delineates "how the work would get done" if you went part-time and then "bring it to your manager," she says. "It could be in the spirit of, 'Let's try this for two months and see if it works.'"

Case Study: Work Collaboratively with Your Team on a Workload Plan

Erin Quinn-Kong, the editor in chief of *Austin Monthly*, found out she was pregnant only a couple of days before her company's new publisher started on the job. She decided to hold off on sharing her news until she was 16 weeks pregnant.

"I have been here five years, but I had a brand-new boss—I wanted to establish a relationship with him before I told him I was pregnant," says Erin, who is due in in a few months.

By the time she told her publisher, Erin had already mapped out a plan for how she would structure her leave and also provided suggestions for how her staff could do the work while she was away. She also talked to her team. "We discussed potentially bringing in someone new at the bottom, but the other editors here decided they wanted to handle it themselves," she says. "We have planned as far in advance as possible, and we're all working hard now to get ahead."

During her leave—which will consist of eight weeks on disability pay and an additional four weeks of both paid and unpaid time off—Erin says she will "go dark" but be reachable to her staff in the event that something important comes up. "I trust them. I know they're good at their jobs, and they're not going to call me for 'in the weeds' type stuff. They will figure it out. It will be a good learning experience for them."

It has also been a good learning experience for Erin. "I've gotten better at delegating since I announced I was pregnant," she says.

When her maternity leave is over, Erin plans to return to her job full-time but will work Wednesdays from home—an arrangement she has already worked out with her publisher. (She started this flextime arrangement at the beginning of her third trimester, which has "really helped with the transition.")

Her daughter will be in day care, one block away from Erin's house. "I will do drop-off, and my husband will do pickup," she says. "That's the plan."

Adapted from "Planning Maternity or Paternity Leave: A Professional's Guide," on hbr.org, May 29, 2015 (product #H0241F).

Understanding Identity as a (New) Working Mother

by Janna Koretz

Quick Takes

- Rethink how you define success
- Acknowledge that you're your own worst critic
- Celebrate your wins—both large and small
- Treat yourself with understanding and flexibility

P arenthood changes you. The roles you used to play, the identities you used to claim—lawyer, dog lover, spin enthusiast—all come second to your new responsibilities. For some, this rearrangement of priorities can lead to a crisis of identity. This is especially true for women, who for both social and neurological reasons tend to feel the split demands of home and work most acutely.[1]

As a clinical psychologist focused on the mental health challenges of people in high-pressure careers, I often read articles and papers about how to get back to "feeling yourself" after becoming a parent. But there are no easy answers, no top-10 lists of tips and tricks that can bring instant comfort and clarity.

Rachel (name has been changed), a longtime therapy client of mine, was a successful trader who had—as far as I could tell—never failed at anything in her life. So, she never anticipated that being a working mother would be something she couldn't handle. Multitasking in a high-stress environment was basically her job description. How hard could it be to add on a few extra tasks at home?

But when Rachel returned to work after maternity leave, she felt as if she was floating, distracted. She couldn't perform to her own standards at the office and felt as if she was dropping the ball at home, too. She had built her identity around her competence and intelligence. Now that all seemed to belong to someone else.

Research into the neurobiology of motherhood has provided some hints about why new mothers often find the return to work so challenging. After giving birth, multiple neurological and structural changes occur that can make it difficult for the new mother to exactly replicate her previous functioning.[2] The brain actually redesigns itself, trimming old connections and building new ones. The result appears to be a brain optimized for "theory of mind"—the ability to understand what others might be thinking and perceiving.

These cognitive and perceptual superpowers helped keep our ancestors alive while living among woolly mammoths. They also give mothers that uncanny ability to analyze their new baby's cries and guess exactly what the infant needs. But the brain doesn't know about our modern work environment; those connections that got trimmed might have been the ones that you relied on to get your job done.

If you're someone who has constructed your adult identity around your career, suffering from "mommy brain" can shake your foundations. Even more unnerving, though, is the sudden instinct some feel to actually want to engage in motherhood above all else. The collision of these two identities, these two seemingly incompatible ways of being—that's the recipe for a good old identity crisis.

Losing your bearings like this isn't just uncomfortable. It can lead to anxiety, depression, burnout, relationship issues, and even substance use. And for most of my clients who are working parents, the chaotic shift to remote work in the time of Covid-19 made things even harder. The boundaries that they once could draw between the household and the office have been blurred, and the human relationships that once gave work meaning have been reduced to a matrix of disembodied, video-chatting heads. No wonder that so many of us feel so unlike ourselves.

Sorting out your identity can be a long and complicated endeavor, but there are two mental rethinks that I often use with my clients to help them figure out how to approach the complicated new world they find themselves in.

Rethink Success

You used to aim for maximum efficiency and effectiveness. Now, you can give yourself a gold star just for survival. You'll have to let a lot go and adjust your definition of success. I guarantee you'll come out ahead if you give yourself credit for all your work on the home front. To do so, try redefining success as getting stuff done both in and out of the office.

Where success might once have meant closing a big client over steaks at a swanky place downtown, it now might mean whipping up breakfast for dinner (ignoring the mess all over the house) as you shout silly songs to your kids giggling in the other room. That client might take an extra day or two to sign, but in the meantime, you've been racking up the wins at home. You're doing way better than you're giving yourself credit for—frame those parenting victories as something to be celebrated.

Rethink Yourself

Our identities go through many changes through the course of our lives. Instead of feeling that your identity has been disrupted, think of it as having been expanded. You were once yourself—now you're yourself, plus something else. There's room to become more.

Parenthood is far from the first time your identity has undergone a shift. Taking on big personal projects like training for a triathlon can often shift our perceptions of ourselves. In that way, adding "parent" to your identity shouldn't require you to abandon old parts of yourself, any more than adding "triathlete" or "great cook" or "photographer" should.

We're often our own most vicious critic. Let go of some of the pressure you're putting on yourself and treat yourself with the understanding and flexibility you'd grant to your best friend. Would you rip your friend for feeding their kids chicken nuggets two nights in a row because something came up at the office? You'd probably laugh about it with them, and then pass the ketchup.

Above all, realize that there are no easy answers, just the hard work in becoming a better (if more complicated) version of yourself. And after you help fight a worldwide pandemic by working from home, answering emails through a soupy brain fog while your toddler is screaming for mustard with their nuggets instead—you'll get there.

Adapted from "New Mothers, Let's Talk About Your Professional Identity Crisis" on hbr.org, August 19, 2020 (product #H05SWO).

Mastering the
Dad Transition

by Bruce Feiler

Quick Takes

- Accept that becoming a father brings a host of emotions

- Find appropriate venues to explore your feelings

- Free yourself from old expectations

- Create new habits at home and embrace a new culture at work

- Update your life story to include the new chapter of fatherhood

Among the transitions people face in their lives, becoming a parent may be the most consequential. The fact that this life change is often expected and joyful does little to reduce the emotional upheaval and personal and professional adjustment required.

But while the transition that new moms face—everything from postpartum depression and career anxiety to a heightened sense of pride and purpose—has been deeply studied by academics and oft discussed in popular culture, the transition that new dads face has been woefully ignored by researchers and reduced to little more than a punchline in popular culture.

Yet the two transitions can't be separated. The impact brought on by massive growth in the number of working moms is inextricably entangled with the impact of having a new culture of engaged dads. As more and more moms have entered the workspace (two-thirds of mothers with children under six work outside the home; for those with children over six, the number balloons to 77%), more dads have entered the parenting space.[1]

Some of this change is by necessity—working moms, by definition, have less time in their day for childcare and increasingly demand that dads step up—but far more of the change is by choice. Dads, it turns out, enjoy being more involved in child-rearing. Asked how they view their role in the family, three-quarters of fathers say their role is "both earning money and caring for my child."

While this flowering of interest in fatherhood has many upsides for dads, moms, and children alike, it raises a host of complications and awkward adjustments for everyone involved, including employers and managers. And though the research into these questions does not go back decades, it has accelerated in recent years.

My own research into life transitions has found that they involve three phases. The first is what I call the "long goodbye," in which the person going through the transition mourns the life they're leaving behind. The second is the "messy middle," in which the person sheds certain habits, mindsets, and lifestyles and begins to create new ones. The third is the "new beginning," in which the person introduces their new self. These phases parallel nicely with the challenges and opportunities new fathers face.

Here, based on this growing body of knowledge, are five tips for new dads to make the transition into working fatherhood a process that's not just life disrupting, but life affirming, too.

Paternity Leave Resources on hbr.org

Paternity leave policies differ from country to country and company to company—and the policies are always changing. If you are expecting a baby soon, hbr.org has many articles about how to prepare for paternity leave, what to do during it, and best practices for when you return to work. We recommend visiting hbr.org and searching for articles on "paternity leave" or "parental leave" to find the pieces that are most relevant to you.

—The Editors

---

1. Accept It

The first lesson for new dads is not to skip over the changes involved. A phase of life has passed. Instead, accept that becoming a father brings with it a host of emotions. These emotions include not just upbeat ones, like joy, elation, and pride, but also downbeat ones, like fear, anxiety, and helplessness.

Researchers in Australia did a comprehensive analysis of more than 500 research papers and found that anxiety disorders in expectant fathers begin in early pregnancy and are widespread across the perinatal period.[2] These feelings crest around birth, when dads often succumb to bouts of helplessness and solitude.[3] For men who already have a history of mental health challenges, these changes can be especially acute.[4]

On top of those emotions at home, dads often feel a sense of concern about falling behind or losing pace at work. Certain routines with colleagues and bosses, from social gatherings to conventions to weekend rounds of golf, may diminish in priority, thereby stoking fears that the responsibilities at home are undermining opportunities at work.

The point is that transitioning to fatherhood is an emotional experience; take time to identify and accept it.

2. Mark It

So how should working dads cope with these feelings?

The answer is to bring the feelings into the open by finding appropriate venues to explore them. My research has found that people use a variety of techniques to respond to the rush of emotions in life transitions: Some write about their feelings; others buckle down and push through. But 80% of people use rituals—public, often shared experiences that indicate to themselves and those around them that they're going through an emotional time and are preparing for what comes next.

The same applies to fathers. For those having a hard time adjusting to the sometimes abstract news of impending parenthood, for instance, the first sonogram has been found to be a galvanizing moment. While the new mom experiences the physical transformation, the dad sometimes needs the visual ritual.

A host of research has also shown that for working dads, sharing stories with others in a support group can help.[5] Even online groups work.[6] The reason such encounters are effective is that gathering with peers in safe settings allows new fathers to normalize their concerns and even use humor to exert some control over them. Expressing these feelings has been shown to lead to completeness, maturity, personal growth, and pride.

The success of such support groups led the Boston College Center for Work & Family to recommend that companies start fathers' affinity groups or offer brown-bag seminars targeted at men as a way to foster acceptance of the dual roles of working dads.[7]

3. Shed It

If the first phase of a life transition is focused on saying goodbye to a past that is not coming back, the second phase, "the messy middle," is concentrated on settling in and adjusting to the new reality. The first step in that process involves giving up old ways.

For working dads, this step means freeing yourself from expectations about your own identity, your relationship with your partner, even your job. A comprehensive study by two scholars in Brazil found that fathers in transition must learn to adjust in four key areas: (1) the father with himself; (2) the father with the mother and the baby; (3) the father with their support network; and (4) the father with his work.

The key finding: Fathers must not overrely on their own fathers as role models, because previous generations of men were less focused on child rearing and balancing work and family. Instead, new fathers must shed these outdated expectations and turn instead to fathers of their own generation who are forging a new set of expectations, habits, and priorities.

Your role model as a working father is more likely to be a colleague or a friend—seek one out.

4. Create It

So what does this new generation of dads want?

The answer to that question may be the most exciting aspect of the working-dad transition. Dads today want a culture, both at home and at work, that embraces hands-on fatherhood. This desire reflects my own research into life transitions, when after saying goodbye to the past and shedding outdated patterns, people in the messy middle turn to astonishing acts of creativity.

In the case of working dads, that means creating new habits at home, from bonding with your baby to coordinating with your partner about what parts of childcare you'll take the lead on. It also means creating a new culture at work that embraces working dads. Make no mistake: Most dads enjoy returning to work. Yet research shows that 98% of them fear losing contact with their babies.

How new dads avoid that fate is by embracing new schedules and new ways of working. More than 75% of dads use flextime when available, 57% work from home at least some of the time (a number that will surely grow as working from home becomes even more prevalent in the wake of the coronavirus pandemic), and 27% use compressed workweeks.[8]

If you're a new dad *and* a manager, take advantage of these programs as a way of helping to normalize and routinize these accommodations and forge a new culture of fatherhood for future generations. As the researchers from Boston College put it: "Offering fathers (and all employees) the time to attend to their personal needs does not offer employees permission to 'slack off.' What it does do is permit them to be more focused and energized when they are working."

5. Tell It

The final phase of a life transition is the "new beginning"; it's the one that arrives at a critical time, when the elation of new fatherhood has passed and the reality of being a dad settles in. The most important skill in this stage: updating the story of your life to include the new chapter of fatherhood.

A life transition is fundamentally a narrative event in which we revisit and update our life story to accommodate a critical change. In this case, becoming a new dad is not just a temporary transition, but a permanent one. And it's not one that ends after a few months, but gets repeated over and over, as a child enters new phases and brings out new responsibilities, as future children come along and tax routines that were already hard won, as new responsibilities accrue at work and pull fathers away from family milestones, and as growing families require big moves, big purchases, and big challenges.

Life transitions are a lifetime sport, and fatherhood just may be the excuse you've long needed to start learning how to play it. But once you do, you'll find that the skills you master are applicable across your life. They can help you turn times that at first seemed overwhelming into times that are filled with affection, wonder, and discovery.

Adapted from "Becoming a Working Dad," on hbr.org, June 16, 2021 (product #H06F3N).

Five Questions New Working Parents Should Ask Themselves

by Jackie Coleman and John Coleman

Quick Takes

- What does each parent actually want?
- What are the financial needs and constraints?
- What roles will each person play?
- Who's losing when?
- How can we stay close to each other?

The demands of both work and parenting are rising. Those employed in full-time work are often working more, but they are also parenting more. Researchers at UC Irvine found that parents in 11 countries spend nearly twice as much time with their kids as they did 50 years ago, with moms spending almost an hour more each day than in 1965 and dads spending nearly an hour each day with kids (as compared with 15 minutes in 1965).[1] Pew has found that dads now see parenting as just as central to their identities as moms do (though moms still parent more), and households with kids are now 66% dual income, versus 49% in 1970.[2] It is no surprise, given these time commitments, that 50% to 60% of parents find work-life balance difficult.

When we decided to start a family years ago, our lives were very different. We slept in. We had more free time. We had different jobs and different working hours. Our financial situation was simpler. Our decision to become parents has been worth every trade-off, but it changed nearly everything in our working and personal lives. We've seen other couples experience the same shifts, through Jackie's prior work as a marriage counselor and John's experience as an executive. And based on that personal and professional experience, we encourage working couples who are new to parenting or are considering becoming parents to start the conversation by asking five questions. These questions are great to ask up front but are worth revisiting over time or when you have additional kids to make sure each person in the relationship is being heard and that your family stays on a firm foundation.

What does each parent actually want?

Men and women now often have more freedom to choose work inside or outside the home. As previously noted, an increasing number of women work outside the home, and according to recent surveys, a small but growing number of men are choosing to raise children full-time.[3] But cultural norms still place immense pressure on a couple. When we had our first child, Jackie originally planned to return to work following a short maternity leave, but ultimately she decided to take an extended period of time to stay home with our children. This was a perfectly valid choice and the one she ultimately wanted to make—but nonetheless she felt enormous pressure to return to work. Conversely, many women would love to pursue their careers but feel pressure to stay at home with children. And men still are often assumed to be better suited to working outside the home, rather than to staying home to raise a family.

Depending on your social circles, there can be overwhelming pressure to prioritize either work or family—navigating an ambitious career or creating flexibility to spend more time with kids. There is no right answer to this question, but there is a right answer for you and your family. And the answer starts with honesty and openness with yourself and each other. What do each of you really want? Ask the question frequently, as the answer may change over time.

What are the financial needs and constraints?

Few of us are free from financial constraints. They are the reality within which we operate. When working parents have kids, a sober evaluation of finances—how much money you want, how much you need, and how much you have—is a foundation for interpreting the constraints under which each family operates. Some people do not have a choice to navigate two-career households, because of childcare needs or health issues, for example, while some must choose the dual-career path due to financial demands. In the United States, each child costs approximately $230,000 to raise—$12,350 to $14,000 per year—and according to Care.com, day care costs more than $10,000 per year, on average, while the average cost of a nanny is more than $28,000 per year.[4] The costs of rearing children are real and meaningful. Each family's financial situation is different, but a clear-eyed evaluation of that situation is critical in order for working parents to properly evaluate the choices they make.

What roles will each person play?

Before having kids (or early on), it is helpful to be clear about who will be responsible for what, while noting that you'll likely also need to be flexible and step in for each other when necessary. Simple division of labor can make day-to-day decisions less stressful. Who pays the bills? Who takes out the trash or does the dishes? Who is responsible for dropping off or picking up the kids from school? Who will stay home from work if the child is sick? Research has shown that frankly working out the division of household labor (particularly if that division is fair) can help eliminate the tendency of "partners to express displeasure toward each other as they completed their chores," and while couples always need to be open to flexibility and helping each other, outlining a mutually understood view of household roles can be extraordinarily helpful in minimizing conflict.[5]

Who's losing when?

Jobs sometimes require moves. Financial needs sometimes require jobs that are not fun. Be honest about who is losing in decisions that require tough choices, and make sure it's not the same person every time.

Relationships require compromise. Decision by decision, one person may have to be prioritized over the other, but over a happy life together, one person cannot lose or win every time. For example, we have witnessed one partner in a relationship receiving a great job offer that requires a move, which may be fine, but when it happens again and again, the partner forced to adapt each time can quickly feel taken advantage of. If one partner feels that they always have to make the trade-offs, they should speak up. And each partner in the relationship must be open to listening to the concerns of the other.

How can we stay close to each other?

While juggling work and kids, it can be easy to neglect your spouse or partner. And if the relationship is failing or festering, both work and kids become infinitely more difficult. It is important to keep your relationship and each individual's mental, physical, and spiritual health prioritized over all else—including over kids and jobs. What will prioritizing your relationship look like, realistically, in the chaos of work and kids? How often will you go on dates? Can you carve out time for meaningful conversation each day? This may mean allotting money for a babysitter for one night per week, spending a day away from work to reconnect with your partner, or finding time to share a long lunch together. Perhaps the most important thing to "solve for" in the complex work-and-family dynamic is each other, and discussing in advance the rules of the road for sustaining your relationship can be essential as the burdens of work and parenting pile up.

Parenting can be remarkably rewarding. The decision to become a parent is not for everyone. But for partners considering the balance of work and parenting—as we have experienced time and time again, both in a marriage counselor capacity and in our personal experience—openly discussing the ways to make that complex dynamic work will lead to happier and healthier relationships and careers. If you and your partner are considering having children or are thinking through your current balance of work and parenting, we encourage you to ask these five questions of each other before you embark on the journey.

Adapted from content posted on hbr.org, May 16, 2018 (product #H04BM6).

Divide Domestic Work Equitably Now—or It May Be Never

by Eve Rodsky

Quick Takes

- New parents should reevaluate how they share domestic work with their partners

- Boundaries establish that each partner's time is equally valuable

- Systems increase efficiency to create time for career, family, and leisure

- Communication about responsibilities should be frequent, carefully considered, and collaborative

- The payoff is a better relationship and more success at work

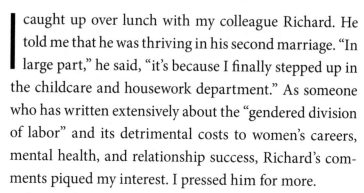

caught up over lunch with my colleague Richard. He
told me that he was thriving in his second marriage. "In
large part," he said, "it's because I finally stepped up in
the childcare and housework department." As someone
who has written extensively about the "gendered division
of labor" and its detrimental costs to women's careers,
mental health, and relationship success, Richard's comments piqued my interest. I pressed him for more.

"In my first marriage, things felt fair *before* kids. I handled dinner because I was the first one home in the evening, my wife would clean up, and we took turns doing
laundry. We never had to discuss the responsibilities of
the home and who does what, and we assumed things
would just go on figuring themselves out when the kids
arrived."

"But kids changed everything," Richard sighed. "Our
roles became lopsided. I made a lot of assumptions based
on *my* job. I unconsciously thought that when I started
working longer hours at the office and since I was earning more, she should take on most of the 'work' at home
and with the kids. Wrong move. She eventually quit her
job to keep up with it all. She resented me and I resented
her for resenting me, and eventually we divorced."

I was all too familiar with this scenario and its supporting research: Mothers are more likely than fathers to make professional sacrifices in deference to child-rearing needs.[1] They're more likely to drop out of the labor force, pass up promotions, and choose occupations that are more family-friendly to accommodate responsibilities at home.

I asked Richard what advice he had for first-time parents or for couples just starting out. He leaned forward and looked me square in the eye. "Get it right the first time."

I thought about Richard's "get it right" advice in the context of the over 500 hetero-cisgender and LGBTQIA+ couples I'd interviewed for my first book, *Fair Play,* a life-management system that more fairly distributes the household workload between partners, and especially partnered couples *with kids.* Richard and his wife were like many of the couples I'd interviewed who had discovered that a "figure it out" approach just doesn't work after children. Why? Because starting with pregnancy and continuing for a decade or more, kids double or triple the amount of domestic labor in a family. Without explicit agreement of who does what, one parent usually becomes the "default," taking on much more of it. And— no big surprise here—it's typically the mother . . . and she suffers at great cost.

The research is stark—on average, a mother's earning power decreases by 5% to 10% for every child she brings into the world due to missed opportunities for promotions, prestigious assignments, pay increases, and bonuses.[2] If you've heard of the "motherhood penalty," this is it. In a 2019 survey, employed moms (50%) were more likely than employed dads (39%) to say being a working parent made it harder for them to advance in their career. Working moms were also more likely than dads to say there had been times where they needed to reduce their work hours (54% vs. 44%) and felt that they couldn't give 100% at work due to parenting responsibilities.[3] Couples' finances suffer as well when women decrease their work hours or are forced out of the paid workforce: They lose hundreds of thousands of dollars in wages and savings.

The Opposite of "Figure It Out"

You don't have to fall into the trap that Richard and his wife did. There is a three-ingredient formula for creating more fulfilled individuals and successful partnerships: *boundaries, systems,* and *communication.* Together, these maximize efficiency and increase fairness, ultimately freeing up both partners to be equally ambitious, committed, and free to pursue who they want to become as professionals *and* grow together as a couple and a family. I've witnessed this shift in countless couples—and in my own marriage.

Boundaries

Setting a true boundary means valuing your time as equal to and as important as your partner's. You each have only 24 hours in a day, and each of you deserves equal time choice over how you spend those hours. If one of you is watching Netflix and catching up on work emails before turning in for the night, while the other is working primarily in service of the household (first scrubbing the cast-iron pan and researching day care options, *then* staying up past midnight prepping for a 9 a.m. client meeting), consider the disparity in how each of you are separately using your time.

Intentional boundary setting means that: (1) you both make explicit that you will honor each other's time as valuable and finite, and (2) a portion of each of your time will be deemed "unavailable"—away from your roles as a partner and new parent and a professional. That's right: Give yourself permission to have uninterrupted time and space just for *you*. This applies to all couples but is particularly important in hetero-cisgender couples, where it has been shown that men do 5 to 10 hours a week *less* housework after a baby comes than they did beforehand and take more leisure time than their partners.[4] Research professor Darby Saxbe of the USC Center for the Changing Family told me, "Women's [leisure] time is more 'contaminated' by interruptions and childcare responsibilities. As an example, if I have a free hour to exercise, I might take my kids to the park or drag them on a hike. Instead of setting a boundary, I bundle family responsibilities with 'my' time."

By putting boundaries around how you and your partner spend time, and consciously choosing to spend it, attitudes and behaviors will begin to shift. "Without those time boundaries," Harvard sociologist Alison Daminger shared with me, "women in particular will continue to perform the bulk of both the cognitive and real domestic labor."

Boundary reframe: My time is as valuable as your time. We both get fair choice over how we use our time at home and at work. Regardless of monetary compensation, our individual "work" is equally valuable.

Systems

The next part of the formula is to put a home organizational system in place that clearly defines who is responsible for every household and childcare task and that sets reasonable expectations for what it looks like to complete those tasks. I refer to this as the CPE (conception, planning, execution) ownership model. Here's a snapshot of how it works:

Your son will eat protein only if he can dip it in French's yellow mustard. In your household, you are responsible for grocery runs, so you notice that mustard is running low. That's *conception*. You add yellow mustard to the grocery list that you create every week. That's *planning*. You go to the grocery store so that yellow mustard (not spicy Dijon) is restocked in your home before you completely run out. That's *execution*.

Women often tell me that they're fed up when domestic expectations aren't met. But a lot of the time, that's due to a couple's failure to divide their tasks and roles clearly and intentionally. In the workplace, our job is to fulfill a specific role and meet individual responsibilities; it should be the same in the "home organization." When each partner agrees to own specific household and childcare tasks and check in each week about those tasks, no one person falls into becoming the meal planner or 2 a.m. bottle feeder by default. For example, my husband owns trash and I own dishes. Each of these requires conception, planning, and execution. We have agreed on the standard that "owning" trash means remembering to take it out every night, replacing the trash bin with a new liner, adding trash bags to the grocery list as needed, and pulling the cart out to the street for pickup.

With ongoing practice and patience, we now trust each other to follow through on every aspect of our individual tasks without reminders or second-guessing. Once both partners understand what is required to meet a responsibility fully, efficiency increases and a sense of fairness arises in place of frustration and resentment. Household tasks don't have to be split evenly—the positive outcomes have more to do with whether a single partner "owns" a task from start to finish.

Systems reframe: To increase efficiency and gain time back to invest in our careers and individual pursuits, we will treat our home as our most important organization.

Communication

Delineating roles and managing expectations cannot happen without communication. This holds true in every professional environment and it's equally important at home. But when I surveyed over 1,000 individuals and asked, "How do you communicate with your partner about sharing domestic responsibilities?" one answer rose to the top: "We don't." Annika, COO of a logistics company, said, "It's too triggering and just leads to me saying, 'I might as well just do it myself.'" The alternative? Twenty-five percent of divorced couples listed disagreements about housework as their top reason for divorce.[5] And despite the common perception that women make out better than men in divorce proceedings, women who worked before, during, or after their marriages see a 20% decline in income when their marriages end.[6] In an effort to avoid these statistics in your own life, engage your partner today in collaborative dialogue with the following three steps:

- **Recognize you are already communicating,** if only nonverbally. Passive-aggressive reminders, silent finger-pointing, grumbling under our breath, and abandoning our partners, literally and emotionally, to figure it out *is* how many of us are communicating. Take it out of the realm of the unspoken and ask directly for what you need.

- **No feedback in the moment.** Instead of demanding help when emotions are high, choose your timing wisely. Wait for it. Couples who give careful consideration to timing, tone, and word choice communicate more effectively—and by extension, they more easily collaborate to create more fairness and efficiency.

- **Communicate regularly.** Make a standing date to check in weekly (or daily, depending on your needs) to talk about the most efficient way to fairly delineate and assign responsibilities.

Ask questions and talk openly. Work as a team to confirm who is handling what. Collaboration is a fluid dynamic and requires ongoing communication.

Communication reframe: Communicate with your partner as you would a colleague at work. Collaborative dialogue requires consistent, intentional practice.

• • •

Before Richard and I wrapped up lunch, I asked what "getting it right the first time" meant to him.

"It means really showing up every day for my wife and kids. I'm an active participant, whereas before I acted like I was waiting to be told what to do. Now, I own my roles just as I do in my professional life. I've become a much better partner and parent to my kids, and my wife has time to pursue her own professional goals. In fact, she was just promoted. A win for us both."

The payoff to getting it right the first time is that when couples intentionally set and exercise time boundaries, put an ownership system in place, and unpack the details of home life through open communication, they're rewarded by more efficiency and greater happiness and harmony at the home. The findings of the *Harvard Study of Adult Development*, a one-of-its-kind, near-80-year longitudinal study on well-being, further shows that good relationships are the *key* to longevity, with study participants identified as "happiest" in their relationships at age 50 later identified as the "healthiest" at age 80. And you'll be looking back, maybe as a grandparent, at a career and a relationship you're proud of.

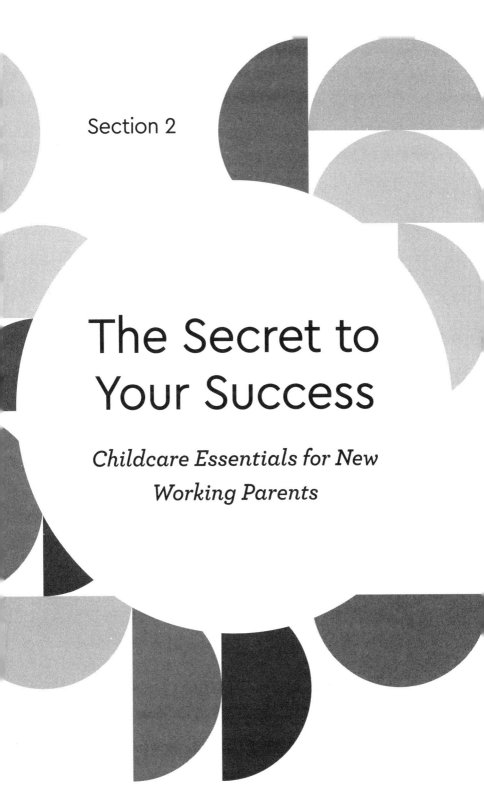

The Secret to Your Success

Childcare Essentials for New Working Parents

A Childcare Primer for First-Time Parents

by Carrie Cronkey

Quick Takes

- Learn about all of the types of care available

- Understand what your family truly needs for care and make trade-offs

- Always have backup care in mind

- Explore and use your parental benefits at work

- If your childcare choice isn't working, make a change

There's so much to do as a new parent, and it often seems like every time you check one thing off your list, five more magically appear. Some are easier to check off than others. More diapers? A few taps on the phone, and they're on their way. Thank-you notes for baby gifts? Maybe we'll finish those tomorrow. There's one item, though, that's on the list of every working parent—and honestly, it will crop up on your list again and again for the next five or 10 years—finding the right people to care for your child when you're working.

I'm a planner, so before my first baby was born, I read several online guides comparing childcare options, and I used their interview checklists when I toured facilities. I called references, checked licensing, and found an in-home day care that I really loved. I was excited! And I thought I had childcare checked off my list. But right before I went on maternity leave, they moved to a new location. I selected a larger center that we came to love, but this change in our childcare plans was the first of many. After our second child was born, we decided to hire a full-time nanny—not only had our family grown, but our professional lives had also changed.

I typically work 10 hours a day, and most years I travel for business almost weekly. My husband's work hours are a bit more flexible, but often require significant travel. With three children ages 10, 8, and 6, it's not possible for us to manage our careers and our family without dependable, affordable childcare—and backup childcare for the times when things don't go as planned.

Just like our family, fewer and fewer people work a traditional eight-hour day anymore, and almost 60% of married families with children are dual income. Figuring out childcare that works the way you do can be overwhelming. But the good news is that there is an array of childcare options, enabling you to select and design a plan that can be tailored for your family's individual needs.

As you learn about these options and how they differ, remember to choose what's best for you, your children, and your family—not what's best for your closest friends, your sister, or your parenting group. Every child and family are different, as are every budget and schedule, so tune out well-meaning advisers. Use this guide to help you find the childcare that suits you best, and come back to it again if and when your needs change.

Types of Care Available

Childcare options include group environments like childcare centers, in-home care like nannies, and an array of choices in between. Here are the basic pros and cons of each.

Childcare centers

At a childcare center, your child will play with and learn from others their age and, in many cases, gain preschool skills. Day care is reliable, licensed, and regulated; provides a daily structure; and helps your child with early development milestones and social skills. But your child may receive less individualized attention, and with more kids, there's also more exposure to germs. And if your child gets sick, they won't be able to attend day care, and it'll fall on you to find backup care (or stay home yourself).

Not all centers offer infant care, and many have strict policies around drop-off/pickup, so there may not be a lot of flexibility for early-morning or late-night meetings or if you're just running late. But they are typically open during holiday weeks and don't close for vacations. If you have an only child, this can be a good option in terms of price and socialization. (See table 6-1, "The cost of care.")

In-home day care

Frequently called family childcare, this kind of day care is located in someone's home, and legally, the carer can

TABLE 6-1

The cost of care

Provider type	Cost for one child*	Cost for two children*
Day care center	$340	$640
In-home day care	$300	$570
Nanny	$612	$654
Nanny share	$404	$404
Au pair	$408	$408
Part-time babysitter (20 hours per week)	$305	$345

Source: Care.com 2021 Cost of Care Survey, https://www.care.com/c/how-much-does -child-care-cost.

*US national average weekly rates.

watch only a handful of children at a time. It's a more family-like setting than centers, the daily schedule and curriculum are usually more flexible, and so are the pickup and drop-off times. However, it's usually managed by just one person, so it's very important that your personalities and childcare philosophies mesh. And if they are sick or out of town, you'll need to find backup care. In-home day care is usually less expensive than a childcare center, as they carry less overhead, but there's more burden on you to do due diligence about licensing, credentials, etc.

Co-op day care

In a co-op, a group of parents creates a schedule and splits the childcare among themselves. Parents structure the activities, curriculum, and playtime, and to make everything work, they must commit time to staffing the co-op. Taking part in a co-op usually involves complex discussions among a larger group of people who all need to agree on standards of care, style, and philosophy, which can be difficult. Co-ops are relatively rare, but they have a big cost benefit if you can make it work. Of course, this option is nearly impossible for families with two full-time working parents, but if you or your partner has a part-time or flexible schedule, a co-op may work for you.

Nannies, nanny shares, babysitters, au pairs

These "in-home care" options provide individualized care in your home. The differences are nuanced and are generally based on the tasks performed and your responsibilities as an employer.

Nannies provide ongoing care throughout the year or for an extended period of time, such as the school year or the summer (often called recurring care). They can be full-time or part-time (after school). Nannies are responsible for your child's care and activities throughout the day, and many have additional responsibilities like meal preparation, children's laundry, and light housekeeping. Because nannies often work exclusively for one family, their hours can match your work schedule and they might even travel with you for family vacations. But you'll also need to cover their sick days, as well as time off. Having a nanny is often a good option for parents of younger children or parents with multiple children, where it starts to make a big difference financially. (See table 6-1.)

With nanny shares, multiple families hire a nanny who watches all the children at once. Typically there are three or four children of varying ages in a nanny share arrangement. In this situation, the nanny earns more but the rate per child paid by the family is often lower than if they had their own nanny. This plan requires families to be on the same page and work together closely given the three-way arrangement.

Au pairs are often students from another country who provide live-in childcare in exchange for room and board with their host family, along with a stipend. They are hired through a licensed agency that can help you through the process. Au pairs may not have extensive childcare experience and therefore might be better suited to slightly older children versus infants. They are typically allowed to work in the country for a prescribed period of time, and as well as room and board, you provide access to a car if you expect them to drive.

Babysitters are typically situational care when you want a night out, need to work late, or have to be in two places at once. You can also use them for after-school care with older children, but they don't usually handle additional tasks like housework or errands.

Whether you choose a nanny, au pair, or babysitter, the best way to prevent disagreements is to create a contract that includes rules and responsibilities, pay and benefits, time off, and more. Explore some sample contracts at Care.com so you don't forget any important details.

Your family

If you're lucky enough to have family nearby, you may be able to find some willing (and free!) childcare, while cementing family bonds and creating great memories. But don't expect them to be the default daily caregiver unless they offer. Be aware that family caregivers can also create unique challenges, such as Grandma wanting to spoil her grandchildren or your sister thinking it's OK to show up late. Take some time to consider issues like rules, schedule, and payment before asking for help. If you have a great relationship with the family member and both of you believe it's a good idea, then you could end up with a wonderful caregiver who already loves your child.

Interviewing Potential Care Providers

Regardless of the type of care you choose, it's essential to do your research and take the process seriously. This is a big decision, and finding the right childcare typically takes about one to three months. But waitlists for childcare centers or finding just the right nanny could make it take longer—so yes, you should probably start looking *before* your baby is born. And even once you've made your decision, be sure to have a plan B so you don't have to scramble like I did!

During the interview process, it may feel uncomfortable to ask the difficult questions, but it's best for you and for them. I often use a third-party interview guide to make this less awkward. I say, "I'm going to use a hiring guide I found online because it helps me make sure I've thought of everything." But add your own questions as well, especially about details of tasks outside the core childcare duties, such as whether they're willing to help with light housework.

Deciding on the Right Type of Care for Your Family

I chose to use a childcare center for my first child, mostly because it was the most cost-effective option. But cost isn't the only factor you should consider when choosing your plan. In addition to knowing your own child and what environment will be best for them, don't forget your own needs, especially when it comes to flexibility.

Since my husband and I both travel for work and my job is demanding, with unpredictable hours, our biggest need when our three children were young was around-the-clock care. That meant a nanny who could do long hours or even overnights. This was a key question in my interviews, and I chose a nanny who had done both for her previous family.

Because we had prioritized flexibility, when my daughter fell off the monkey bars in kindergarten and broke her arm, I didn't stress over the fact that my husband was out of town and couldn't get home in less than 24 hours. I was able to be at the hospital with my daughter during her surgery and stay overnight while my nanny was at home with my 1- and 3-year-old children. This was invaluable for our family.

Each option has its own strengths and weaknesses, so make sure you know your must-haves and be willing to compromise on your nice-to-haves. You're going to hear stories about nannies who cook gourmet meals while the baby is napping and day care centers that have every child reading before kindergarten. But they'll probably fall short in other areas. There's no "perfect" care provider, so be honest with what you need and respect the trade-offs.

Once you've figured out what you need, deciding what type of care you'll use and who will be the provider becomes easier.

Choosing the Best Provider for the Kind of Care You Want

If you've decided to send your child to a childcare facility, consider each option's proximity to your home and work, and which is more important for you. Visit your top choices in person so you can meet the director and caregivers. Ask about employee training and certifications, turnover, and the ratio of children to adults, as well as what background checks they run.

If you've chosen to hire an in-home caregiver, we recommend starting with a phone or video interview and then an in-person interview. Care.com and countless other parenting sites provide free interviewing resources online. If you're interested in the candidate, do a background check (unless the platform or service you're using has already done so) and call at least two prior references to ask them tough questions.

Once you've checked references, do a trial run. Send your child to the childcare center for a few hours or have the potential nanny spend time with your kids for several hours while you're home. If your children are old enough, get their opinion afterward. And regardless of the type of care, please pay the caregiver for their time.

Employer-Sponsored Care

Slowly but surely, more employers are stepping up to help their employees manage the demands of parenting. There are a variety of programs out there, so be sure to check with your HR department to find out what care benefits are provided. Many people miss this step, especially if they are making childcare decisions while on parental leave.

Access to care, backup care, support services

Some businesses will pay for their employees to have memberships on sites like Care.com so they can find the care they need. All the planning in the world doesn't matter when your child is sick and can't go to day care, your nanny is sick and can't come in, or it's a school holiday but you're working. Any of these scenarios prevent you from getting to work, which is why many employers now subsidize backup care—both in-center and in-home—for their employees. Some go even further with other support services. Check with your employer about which of these are available to you:

- Lactation support for specific breastfeeding challenges

- Breast milk shipping for moms who travel for work

- On-demand tutoring and study tools for employees and family members

- Resources to help successfully transition back to work after maternity or paternity leave

Care specialists

Employers are also finally understanding that one size does not fit all when it comes to care support. Many now offer personalized assistance, sometimes through an employee assistance program, that support mental health or overall well-being for everything from small, daily problems to major life events, such as:

- Pre/postnatal resources

- Adoption support

- Finding special needs programs

On-site and subsidized daily care

On-site childcare is also offered by some larger employers, but space is limited and there's typically a waitlist. So as soon as you know you're expecting, you should ask HR about the details. Finally, a handful of companies will now simply provide a childcare subsidy for parents to spend as they wish. Be sure to ask about that too!

Nothing Is Permanent—If Your Childcare Isn't Working, Make a Change

My most important childcare advice is to trust your instincts. If the situation doesn't feel right to you, then it's not right and you should make a move—children are very adaptable. If your first choice seemed great in theory but turns out to not be the right fit in reality, it's OK to make a change—even if it's right away. I know one family whose first nanny lasted just two weeks, but their second one has been with them for seven years. Even if you're lucky enough to get it right the first time, don't be afraid to make a switch as your family grows and changes.

My second most important piece of advice is don't get too far ahead of yourself. The right solution today may not be the right solution in six months, one year, or two years, so don't try to solve for that. Solve for right now. While it's important to find what best fits your family *now*, don't feel committed to this decision for the next five or 10 years.

You have a long way to go before you'll cross childcare off your to-do list once and for all. Until then, know all your options, think creatively—and always do what's best for your family.

Questions to Ask Yourself When Working with an In-Home Caregiver

by Daisy Dowling

Quick Takes

- Your partnership with an in-home caregiver will be unlike any other working relationship

- Talk openly and honestly with your caregiver about what's important to you

- Integrate your caregiver into your support network

- Understand how much of your "work self" you want to bring to the relationship

- Make sure the caregiver feels respected, engaged, and heard

You're no newbie when it comes to working relationships: You've collaborated with and maybe even managed colleagues effectively for years. But now you're hiring a babysitter for an afternoon, or you're bringing on a full-time nanny or au pair when you return from leave, or the grandparents are taking the baby for the weekend so you can *finally* get a real night of sleep. And while developing a great collaboration with that in-home caregiver feels like it *should* be easy, let's face it—it isn't. Sure, you agreed on the sitter's hours or the au pair's start date, but actually having a new adult around your home is a different thing. It may feel strange or awkward, and the workplace relationships you're used to forging aren't centered around the most precious thing in the world to you, your 6-month-old. So this partnership feels fundamentally *different* than any you've handled—and it is. You're in the position of manager, CEO, and chief security officer, and yet you want to have a warm, happy, family-type relationship with your caregiver at the same time. You could be the world's best professional collaborator, but the setting and stakes are different now, and your feelings and level of confidence are different too.

Don't resign yourself to awkwardness, though, or beat yourself up with a "I should be able to figure this out!" Instead, ask yourself the following questions. As you mull over your answers, you'll be able to get things sorted: to map out the path to a good, healthy relationship with your child's caregiver and remain calmly assured in your role as parent along the way.

1. What are your apprehensions around starting and using in-home care?

No matter how glowing the new sitter's references were, it's natural to be worried about entrusting your baby to someone new—or to be concerned that they'll be spending x number of hours per week with someone who isn't *you*. But those kinds of worries are actually proof of your commitment as a parent, and of how well bonded you are to your child. Despite these concerns, if you call these emotions out directly, they'll lose some of their power over you—and you may even begin to see ways to work around them. For example, admitting to yourself that you are worried "the baby will know the sitter better than she knows me!" may prompt you to find better ways to stay connected with them during your workday. Or it may help you resolve to talk to other working parents who have dealt with these feelings themselves. Itemize your concerns—and then think through how to diffuse them.

2. Is the help you're using *negotiated or paid*?

You'll likely need to adjust your approach depending on whether a friend or family member is providing their services for free or you're paying a nanny or sitter the market rate. If you're keen to keep the baby on a certain sleep schedule, you may be able to politely ask, or respectfully direct, a paid caregiver to do so—but may have to do more explaining, convincing, or even cajoling to get a volunteer helper on board. Having your own parent or an in-law taking care of your child can be a wonderful, reassuring setup—but you may also find yourself in a lower-control, "Grandma knows best" situation when it comes to nap schedules. Think ahead about when and how often you'll defer to Grandma's judgment—and when you'll insist your rules are applied consistently.

3. Have you talked openly and honestly with your caregiver about what's most important to you?

What's most important might be your family's faith practices or cultural values or a certain health concern. It may also be keeping the kids away from screens or their getting a certain amount of sleep each day—or your desire to keep them out of the den, where you keep your vintage guitars. Maybe the most important thing is that your caregiver arrives each morning early enough for you to make the 8:00 a.m. team meeting. Most likely, it's some combination. You get the point: Your sitter isn't clairvoyant, so talk about what matters most—and do so right up front.

4. How well have you integrated your caregiver into your broader network of helpers and supporters?

If it "takes a village to raise a child," then the more connected a caregiver is to that village, the easier it is to be sure your childcare arrangement is working the way you want. Don't just provide the caregiver with emergency contact information—introduce them to important relatives and family friends, coach them on how to plug into your broader network of support when you're traveling for work, and so on.

5. How much of your "work self" do you want to bring into interactions with your caregiver?

Force yourself to really think about it by answering on a scale of 1 to 10. You're trying to strike a new, unique tone here, one that's between "leader" and "family." There's no right or wrong answer, but your child's nursery isn't a conference room, and it's better to be deliberate and intentional rather than making up your new approach on the fly. Think ahead as to how to soften your conversational style; provide more—and more-positive—feedback than you would to a regular colleague; share more information about yourself and your own vulnerabilities than you would at work; and encourage them to share their own feeling and concerns with you.

6. What does your overall keeping-in-touch and information-sharing system look like?

Good communication is the basis of any good relationship. You'll want to have your communications operating system—your "when, how, why, and what"—carefully mapped out here. For example, you might ask them to send a picture of your child every couple of hours—both to warm your heart and for your general peace of mind. You could schedule an extra 15 minutes together each Friday afternoon to compare notes about how your son did throughout the week, always call home at midday to see how your toddler is getting on, or agree that any time he falls off the tricycle merits an immediate call to Mom or Dad. What you're aiming for here is to feel that there's a clear, sufficient, unhurried, and constructive back-and-forth.

7. Is your sitter getting enough time for rest and renewal?

It's wonderful if a grandparent is helping out at home—but their own age, or limits, may make it hard for them to look after your toddler for long uninterrupted stretches. And just as you need downtime to function at your best at work, your caregiver—whoever they are—will need the same. At the start of any new relationship, think about reassuring the sitter that you want them to take breaks when the baby naps—or ask your current caregiver when they plan to use their vacation.

8. How are you expressing appreciation?

If the care arrangement is working out just as you'd hoped or you see the nanny as a member of "team family," that's a wonderful reassuring feeling—and important for them to know. So consider saying so, and being direct: "From our perspective, the past two months have gone incredibly well, and we appreciate all the care you're providing." Like any colleague, caregivers will feel happier, more loyal, and more motivated when they know you value their contributions.

9. How would you feel if your roles were switched?

Would you feel respected, engaged, appreciated, and listened to? Would words like *mutual, collaborate,* or *partnership* feel on point? Remember: While starting in-home care of any kind means taking a practical and personal leap yourself, the caregiver you're relying on—whether they're a local teenager, a full-time nanny, or your own mom—is as much a three-dimensional, hardworking person as you are, and you want to do right by them.

Adapted from Workparent: The Complete Guide to Succeeding on the Job, Staying True to Yourself, and Raising Happy Kids *(product #10309E), by Daisy Dowling (Harvard Business Review Press, 2021), chapter 2, "Care."*

Creative Strategies from Solo Parents on Juggling Work and Family

by Marika Lindholm

Quick Takes

- Capitalize on "stolen moments" to work or to connect with your kids

- Consider unique housing arrangements

- Arrange atypical work schedules

- Build a pragmatic support network

The daily challenge of feeding, caring for, and educating children is tough. Add the stress of earning enough money to sustain the family's well-being and feeling fulfilled in your own career, and it becomes daunting. And solutions that work for each unique family can be hard to come by.

For solo parents—those who are single, divorced, widowed, or have partners away from home due to deployment, incarceration, disability, a health condition, or work—the challenge is that much harder. Whether it's staying up late with a feverish child, needing to stay longer at work, coping with a sudden emergency, enforcing house rules, or tackling the myriad mundane decisions that arise throughout the day, a solo parent does it alone. But knowing it's all up to you can also be a profound, and often empowering, responsibility.

After my divorce, I became more self-reliant, creative, and flexible in my parenting because I had to step up and make it work. As the founder of ESME.com (Empowering Solo Moms Everywhere), I've learned that this ingenuity isn't unusual—solo parents often develop unique problem-solving skills in response to their unique situations.

Here are just a few that I've observed through my own experience and in talking to a variety of single parents that *all* working parents can learn from as they navigate work and family.

Capitalizing on Stolen Moments

Time is a solo parent's enemy—there aren't enough hours in a day. Because of this, solo parents must identify where they can save time and prioritize what's most important. They know they are not able to do it all and that something has to give, whether it's a messy house, an extra hour of screen time for the kids, a shortened dog walk, or takeout for dinner (none of which impact their family's well-being). Aware that time is a precious commodity, solo parents take advantage of small moments to connect with their children, fulfill their work responsibilities, and make the most out of their time by squeezing work and personal tasks into commutes, sports practices, waiting rooms, and odd hours. Solo mom and writer Joni Cole notes, "You can achieve good work in half-hour increments, and they add up."

Figuring out ways to remain productive without busy-work and long hours, solo parents challenge long-held assumptions about workplace efficiency and dedication. Moms who have to squeeze in a school pickup or dads who need to work from home when a child is sick are equally dedicated as workers with partners—perhaps even more so. Parenting alone inspires a healthy reframing of one's relationship to work that is liberating, rewarding, and instructive to those of us who need a reminder of what's important.

Setting Up Unique Housing Arrangements

A solo mom in Los Angeles posted recently to our single moms' group: "I am a single mom of two teenage daughters, and one is going off to college. I am interested in finding another single mom who would be interested in renting together. . . . Maybe we have opposite parenting schedules?"

The traditional nuclear family arrangement doesn't always support solo parent families well—financially or logistically. To lower housing costs and get help with childcare, many solo parents share homes and rentals or move in with extended family. Atlanta mom Kaleena Weaver explains, "I bought a house with a basement unit so my mom could move in. I cover all the bills, and she helps with the kiddo and household work." Janelle Hardy, a single mom from Canada, opted to rent a large house so she could take in a roommate or two who enjoy being part of a family environment. Hardy also took part in exchange student programs to offset costs and have an extra set of hands while raising her children. Another mother, Lisa Benson, uses part of her home to rent out as an Airbnb for extra income.

While parents can often set up extended family or friendship households organically, a national organization called Coabode can help.[1] Their mission is to "connect single mothers whose interests and parenting philosophy are compatible, with the purpose of sharing a home and raising children together." In addition to the clear psychological and financial benefits, sharing a home with another family helps solo parents solve many of the logistical issues that come with raising children on their own, such as how to cover days off from school.

Arranging Atypical Work Schedules

After his wife passed away, Conrod Robinson changed jobs to be closer to home:

> I cut my commute time by more than half so I could make after-school events, cook dinner at home, etc. This allowed me to leave for work at around the same time my son left for school in the morning. I took a sizable cut in compensation to do that, but I'm glad I made the decision to spend more time at home.

Although not all solo parents have to sacrifice higher pay and upward mobility to be more available to their children, many do opt for night shifts, flextime, and part-time work. Increasingly, organizations understand that flexibility results in a more dedicated workforce, and thus today's solo parents, more than ever, are able to create schedules around their family's needs.[2]

Sometimes such choices can mean creating new career paths. "I quit my job as a social worker to offer childcare in my home so I could stay home with my children and pay my bills," says solo mom Heidi Kronenberg. "I loved being home with my son and daughter, and they enjoyed having other children around." Once both children were in elementary school, Kronenberg returned to social work and then ultimately started her own business focused on behavioral health and counseling. "My experience with in-home childcare provided skills that translated well to starting a business," explains Kronenberg.

Working from home is another strategy that solo parents employ to ease the daily juggle—whether that's a few times a week or a fully remote position. Shantell Witter, a "mompreneur" in Atlanta, made the decision to home-school so that she could sustain her multiple businesses, including Only with Love Books, a BIPOC-focused bookstore for families, and two education-oriented businesses. By merging her business interests with her desire to homeschool, Witter achieves a fulfilling balance.

Building Pragmatic Support Networks

Solo parent creativity extends beyond time management and unique work arrangements. I've been amazed at some of the clever ways that solo parents alleviate some of the work/family grind by building support networks—some of which include their own children. Former solo mom Cheryl Dumesnil recalls,

> When my kids were tweens, if I had to work uninterrupted in my home, I would tell them I would pay them each $5 to babysit the other. The catch was each kid got to tell me if his babysitter sibling deserved to be paid. Cheapest childcare ever! I'd get three to four hours of work done for $10.

I myself used to have the kids "play chef" one night a week, where they made dinner. They thought it was fun, and I had time to get some extra work done. What's more, evidence suggests that children of solo parents are more resilient and self-sufficient because they are expected to participate in household tasks rather than just do chores.[3]

In-person and virtual networking are also critical for solo parents. The most impactful networks are a blend of close connections and people you don't know that well: Friends and family offer meaningful bonds, while acquaintances give you access to information you might not get from your inner circle. A close-knit group of parents might know all the same babysitters and after-school programs, while those outside your circle may know about resources you wouldn't otherwise hear about, such as a new or little-known program in a neighboring town. The same is true for Facebook and other online support groups. The more varied the network, the more diverse information you have access to.

Your community and network can also alleviate some of the stress of daily meals and errands. A once-a-week potluck not only takes the burden off dinner that night but also allows for connection and support. Food exchanges with friends solves the interminable question, "What's for dinner?" Teaming up with another parent while shopping, running errands, or just spending time at the playground is another effective strategy. Solo mom Chaya Beyla suggests, "Asking a friend to ride around with you while you run errands provides socialization *and* someone to wait in the car with your sleeping toddler while you rush into the store, bank, or post office." You can also set up clothing swaps, childcare, and carpooling in your network.

Despite all the obstacles, working parents without partners at home have figured out how to make the most out of their time, home and work lives, and networks.

Through unique and creative problem solving, they've found new ways to press forward and be the best parents they can be under challenging circumstances.

Adapted from "Creative Strategies from Single Parents on Juggling Work and Family," on hbr.org, April 8, 2021 (product #H06AAG).

Section 3

Old Job, New You

Returning to Work After Parental Leave

How to Transition Back After Parental Leave

by Rebecca Knight

Quick Takes

- Resist taking your emotional temperature too early in your return

- Make your schedule as predictable as possible, but prepare for the unexpected

- Seek out support and encouragement from other parents at work

- Do practice runs with your caregiver

- Ask for flexibility if it will help you do your job better

- Don't assume that you will be the same professional you were before you became a parent

Transitioning back to work after parental leave is hard. You've been out of the flow of the office for weeks or months, and you're returning as a different person with new priorities and concerns (not to mention the stress and strain of endless new logistics). It's jarring and often overwhelming. So how can you make your first few weeks back in the office as smooth as possible? If you have the choice, is it better to ease back slowly or to jump right in? How should you manage your relationships with your boss and coworkers? Perhaps most important, where can you go to get the emotional support and encouragement you need during this time?

What the Experts Say

Returning to work after being home with a new baby is "a transition that's like no other," says Daisy Dowling, the founder and CEO of Workparent, a consulting firm for working parents and employers. "Everything is changing—from your practical day-to-day schedule, to your new responsibilities as a parent, to your identity in terms of how you've seen yourself your entire adult life," she says. Adding to the pressure, you're making this transition while "taking care of a little human who might not be sleeping very well." It's an "intense physical and psychological adjustment," adds Denise Rousseau, a professor of organizational behavior and public policy at Carnegie Mellon University. "You may not feel ready to leave your child," she says. You may even feel guilty about your decision to go back to work in the first place. "All of this is normal," of course, but that "doesn't make it any less overwhelming." Reentry is a challenge, and there's no perfect path. Have faith "that you will walk it well," she says, and know that there are many ways of doing so. Here are some pointers for how to navigate those first weeks back at work.

Be gentle with yourself.

First things first: "Try not to take your emotional temperature in the first two to three weeks" that you're back on the job, says Dowling. Your life has changed dramatically. "You will be tired, frustrated, and full of self-doubt" she says—maybe even conflicted about whether to return to work or stay at home. Indeed, many people come back from parental leave and consider quitting. But just because you're sad or worried now doesn't mean you will be forever, she says. "It's an emotional time." Remind yourself that it's too early "to draw conclusions." Don't ignore your feelings, but bear in mind that, just like the ages and stages of your new child, this too shall pass. "Don't be too hard on yourself," agrees Rousseau.

Consider your schedule.

Making the transition back to work will never be easy," but there are "a lot of aspects of it that you can manage and plan for," according to Dowling. Take, for instance, the question of whether you return gradually by working a couple of days a week or resume full-time work from the get-go. Not everyone has an option, but if you do, it's sensible to consider the pros and cons of each.

- **Easing back in by working part-time at first** "allows you to learn how to do the job you did before differently," says Rousseau. It removes some of the pressure of juggling your new home life, and it helps you focus at work. "You learn to prioritize and concentrate on the things that move the needle." When you're part-time, "you can't putz around," she says. "You have to be discriminating" about the tasks you take on and how you do them. Be aware, however, that this schedule might "send a complex message" to your team, says Dowling. "If you've been a guns-blazing professional and you come back to two days a week, you're telegraphing—even if you don't mean to—that you are no longer working in the same way," she says. "Your attention and ambition have shifted."

- **Going back full-time immediately** allows you to "resume the career you had before," rather than one "with radically reduced expectations," says Dowling. It may be harder at first, but the benefit is that you're not "setting the bar differently" at the outset. Returning full-time allows you to "go in and do some data gathering and test things out." If you need to, you can then "ratchet back."

Whichever path you choose, Dowling recommends working only two or three days in your first week back on the job. A midweek start allows you to make the adjustment a little more slowly and ensures that you don't have a five-day stretch of work from the start, which will no doubt feel too long.

Do a few practice runs.

Returning from parental leave often involves executing on a new set of complicated logistics. Dowling advises "trying to get ahead of them" as much as possible to "minimize the sting." Start with the basics: The first day you go back to work shouldn't be the first day your baby goes to day care or stays home with a new nanny. Dowling recommends doing at least a few practice drop-offs or asking your sitter to start a week early. "Get your child used to the process and accustomed to the caregiver," she says. Dry runs will help you, too. "Get up in the morning, take a shower, put on your work clothes, feed the baby, take her to day care, get your Starbucks, and drive to the office," she says. "Then literally turn right back around." If you're nursing, try to add a pumping session or two in there as well. Your goal, says Rousseau, is to get "a realistic preview" of what to expect.

Be up front with your boss.

Maybe not on your first day back, but at some point, you need to have an honest and "up-front conversation" with your boss about the new realities of your life as they relate to your job, says Dowling. Acknowledge that the "next few weeks may be bumpy"—your emotions may be all over the map—but make it clear that "you are still fully committed to your job and organization." Think about what you need from your employer and how to make your new situation work best for you. Bring up "projects you'd like to be considered for" and "work travel that you're willing to do or not do," Dowling adds. "You need to proactively own your story; the more you can control, the better." Rousseau recommends asking for your boss's advice and counsel on how to reenter successfully. Be candid and realistic about what can be accomplished in your first few weeks and months back on the job. "Talk to your manager about what's critical versus what's nice to have."

Set expectations with colleagues.

Be mindful of how you manage relationships with colleagues as you settle into your new work life. A lot of parents return from leave with the "mindset of 'I'll figure it out' or 'I'll adapt,'" but this is risky, Dowling says. "If you don't go in with a clear idea of what your schedule and plans are, others will make assumptions." Communication is critical. Be direct about how and when you will work. Make your schedule predictable. For instance, "if you need to leave every night at 5 p.m. on the dot, then people will know not to come by your office at 4:59 p.m. wanting to talk," she says. Things may change over time and even on the fly, of course, but if you "train your colleagues on what to expect"—and explain your schedule requirements clearly—they will learn how and when to adjust as needed.

Seek support.

Resuming your professional life is a process—don't go it alone. As you make the transition, Dowling advises, seek out support and encouragement. "Join a mom and dad network," she says. Look for an online support community. "Build connections with people in your neighborhood who also have young children." Find out if your employer has resources for new parents. Seek advice from colleagues who've been through the process.

Be deliberate about your time with your child.

As you're getting back into the swing of work, think about "how you will spend time with your kids," Dowling says. Will it be in the morning? In the evenings? Mostly on weekends? Especially "if you work long hours or travel," you need to have a plan for when you'll have "rewarding time with your child." Let your child's caregiver in on your thinking. Whether the baby is going to day care or staying at home with a nanny or family member, these people are now critical pieces to your professional puzzle. "Do you want them to send pictures to you while you're at work? Will you do FaceTime?" The bottom line is, "Don't allow your emotional bond with your child to play second fiddle," Dowling says. "Be deliberate."

Reset your expectations.

In those early days of coming back to work, it's wise to think about how you can recast yourself professionally. Think about "what makes you special or different," Dowling says. Then consider how to modify those attributes to suit your new life. "If you were the hardest-working person in the office, then maybe you become the most efficient. If you were the best mentor or project leader, you become the best delegator," she says. Your goal is to reset your expectations for yourself. "If you don't, you will find yourself trying to resume a role you can no longer play." Rousseau agrees: "You need to be realistic about what you can and should give."

Case Study: Set Expectations with Others While Leaving Room for Flexibility

Courtney Lazzari's first maternity leave in 2014 involved a lot of change. During her time away, Courtney, a partner at EY, relocated from New York to Texas and got promoted to a new role. "I was a new mom in a new job in a new city. At the time, I thought, 'Let's make all these transitions at once,'" she says with a laugh.

As Courtney geared up to return from leave, she thought about what she wanted to achieve in her new position. She also reflected on her identity at EY. "In New York, [my colleagues] knew me and my work ethic," she says. "In Houston, I didn't have a historical relationship with them. I wanted to make sure people still thought of me as hardworking. I was anxious not to be viewed as someone whose priorities had shifted."

When she returned to work, she had a direct conversation with her manager to discuss her goals for the job.

They also talked about expectations—both what her boss wanted to see from her and what she needed from the organization as she adjusted to her life as a mother.

Courtney expressed her commitment to the company and her job. But she also acknowledged that she needed more flexibility than in the past. "My one nonnegotiable was that I needed to always be able to take my son to the doctor—whether it was a planned appointment or if he was sick. I was up front that I would up and leave whatever I was doing in order to do that."

In addition, Courtney talked to her boss about her schedule and how she would structure her day. Initially, she planned to start her workday at 7 a.m. so that she could leave at 3 p.m. to spend time with her son. She then planned to log back in at night once he went to bed.

She did this for a while. But Courtney, who has a one-hour commute each way, soon found that this schedule was not sustainable. Now, "I work from home two days per week," she says. "It just gives me more moments in the day to be a mom." (She now also has a daughter.)

Still, she's glad she tried to resume her old schedule because it helped her recognize that, while it wouldn't work over the long term, she still wanted to have a career. Her advice to others: "Don't force yourself into a bad decision."

Adapted from "How to Return to Work After Taking Parental Leave" on hbr.org, August 2, 2019 (product #H052W1).

When Returning to Work, Focus on Three Things

by Avivah Wittenberg-Cox

Quick Takes

- Build your sense of self by aligning with your partner on parenting, careers, and caring

- Communicate with your boss and lobby for what you need

- Understand the corporate culture you're in and pace yourself

A few years ago, I spoke at a bank's women's conference. One of the women there enthused, "I'm so grateful about the bank's return-to-work program for mothers." "Why are you grateful?" I asked. She looked bemused by my question. "Isn't your company saving money by getting a skilled employee back rather than having to recruit and train a new one?" I pressed. "Won't they be able to serve you up as a role model to a generation of talented parents-to-be coming along behind you?"

Most new parents don't see themselves in this positive light, especially in the United States. Instead, they feel guilt.[1] Guilt and gratitude for the most basic management of a simple human reality—people having children.

While you may not be able to fix the system you're in, you *can* nudge it forward by making a concerted effort to focus on three things when you return to work: your sense of self, your boss, and your corporate culture. Strategically managing all three will not only make your own journey a lot easier, but you'll also contribute to adapting your company to 21st-century realities.

Build your sense of self by aligning with your partner.

There's no denying that leaving the workplace for any-thing from a few weeks to a few years can give your sense of self a hit. In addition to not sleeping through the night and the steep learning curve of suddenly adjusting to being responsible for a fragile and helpless human, new parents inevitably feel that they are out of the loop at work. They often feel out of the loop of life, period.

The more intense and fast-paced the workplace cul-ture, the more people feel they are speeding backward to-ward irrelevance. Don't let yourself believe this. There are many roads to developing a career. If you have a partner, aligning your goals with them is the first essential step.

Dual-career couples need to craft a plan for an over-arching, shared life vision, of which two mutually en-hancing career plans are a part. If you stick to trying to manage two independent career tracks, you risk end-ing up competing rather than collaborating. That's a guaranteed confidence killer. It's also not great for your relationship.

There are three chapters to the conversations you need to have with your partner:

- **Parenting:** What kind of parents do you each want to be? Primary, secondary, shared? This may seem obvious, but too many couples make assumptions based on their cultures, their parents, or their social circles. Make it explicit. Your future depends on it. Don't suddenly discover, as a mentee of mine did, that her surgeon husband's idea of coparenting was the occasional Sunday afternoon in the park.

- **Careers:** What kind of career do you each aim for? What are the short-, medium-, and long-term goals? What are the career patterns of the next decade in each existing career? Pace yourself—and your partner—for the long haul. If you design it well, you can both have it all—but maybe not both at the same time, or not all at once.

- **Caring:** What's your support network look like? Who will back you up and who will manage them? What are plans B and C? Can you rely on family, on outsourcing, or on friends? It takes a village, remember. Don't even think you'll survive this phase without help. Ask for it, plan for it, design it in. Then comanage it.

The mistake too many returning parents make is a mixture of perfectionism and impatience. They want to do too much and be perfect in all dimensions—a perfect professional, a perfect parent, a perfect partner. This leads to almost guaranteed burnout. Forget perfect.

Relax, breathe deeply, and prepare for a marathon, not a sprint.

Communicate with your boss and lobby for what you need.

Once you've got your plan and you're pacing down with your partner, it's time to start building a communications plan for your boss.

If you're in a male-dominated organization, most bosses are not yet totally comfortable managing conversations about balancing babies and ambitions with the growing number of smart, young women coming up the pipelines. And they're even less so with the growing number of men who want to be involved fathers, especially if they themselves "sacrificed" (usually their word) their personal lives to their careers. Aside from a limited number of progressive workplaces, the onus falls on you to manage the process.

Some managers will make well-meaning assumptions about returning parents, trying to spare them from challenging assignments. Others will, on the contrary, want to test whether you're still "ambitious" and offer you a promotion in . . . China. In either case, you'll need to manage up and lobby clearly for the roles or promotions you're expecting—or the limits you're setting. Don't expect your boss to understand your inner thoughts or resolve the inevitable conflicts. Pitch a pace, a plan, and a solution. Then check in regularly.

And remember: Whatever your manager's response, forget gratitude. If you're a woman, keep in mind that women comprise almost 60% of university graduates and at least half the incoming talent pool in most companies. You're the future—help your bosses learn how to manage you better. If you're a man, know that you're a necessary role model to leveling the playing field for both men and women. Educate older men in the changing perspectives of the next generation and the flexibility that technology is opening up for everyone.

Understand the corporate culture you're in and pace yourself.

The systems and cultures of firms today still assume that 24/7, up-or-out, linear careers are the default setting—the norm. Everything else, including the 86% of women between 40 and 44 who will have had children is a deviation that companies are grudgingly catering to.[2] Not to mention the majority of men who now live in dual-earner couples and are finding it particularly awkward to report to men of the previous generation who are wondering what kind of men want to look after *children*?

Some companies have great policies, but managers who aren't very open to applying them. Make sure you know the corporate rules of the game in your company. If they're unclear, reach out to other colleagues with kids.

The policies are often in place, but behaviors lag a generation behind. Two-thirds of men would take parental leave if they thought it wouldn't negatively impact their career.[3] But times are changing fast. Both men and women need to be part of the change we all want to see.

So enlist your partner, sign up your boss, and put on your marathoner's shoes. Kiss your beautiful baby goodbye at day care drop-off (they'll be just fine) and enjoy the extraordinary satisfactions of mindfully choosing to manage both your family and your career.

Adapted from "When Returning to Work, New Parents Should Focus on 3 Things," on hbr.org, March 6, 2019 (product #H04TP2).

How to Negotiate Remote and Flexible Work Arrangements

by Ruchi Sinha and Carol T. Kulik

Quick Takes

- Flexibility includes *what* you do, not just where and when
- Your company doesn't need to have an explicit flex policy for you to negotiate flexible work
- Understand your company's policies before you make the ask
- Document your remote and flexible successes
- Have a backup plan in place

S hould you consider "making the ask" and negotiating remote and flexible work arrangements with your boss? If so, how do you go about it?

First, let's look at the two myths about negotiating flexible work arrangements.

Myth 1: Negotiating flexibility is mainly about when and where you do your work.

There is a tendency to view flexibility negotiations as revolving only around the hours you work and the location from which you work. But flexibility is also determined by the nature of the tasks that make up your job role. Some tasks are better performed remotely than others. When you negotiate flexibility, you need to also negotiate what work you will do, how your work fits into the bigger picture, and how it will be evaluated.

One way to do so is "job crafting." It is a process of arranging your work responsibilities to better fit your needs, strengths, and passions. When you negotiate your tasks or role with your boss, think about the scope of your tasks and responsibilities, as well as the logistics of how you will interact and coordinate with other members of your team, and how you and your team's role performance and objectives will be monitored and evaluated.

It is within these conversations that you can bring up the feasibility and effectiveness of flexible work—laying the groundwork to negotiate where and when you work. For example, you might make a case to bundle certain tasks and deliverables in a way that allows you to complete them away from the office, or you might take up some new responsibilities and give away others to shape your role to suit your flexible work schedule.

Myth 2: Negotiating flexibility is *only* possible when your organization has an explicit policy supporting flexible work.

Research shows that employees can adopt three different strategies for negotiating work flexibility—asking, bending, and shaping.[1]

Asking is easy when your company already has a clear organizational policy for you to work remotely. You simply "ask" your manager.

Bending is a negotiation strategy when you ask for flexibility as an exception to the rule. Your organization may not have a flexibility policy, or you may want a specific type of flexibility for which there is no policy and no precedent.

Shaping is a type of negotiation where you attempt to change the organizational policy by making a flexibility case not just for yourself but for a larger collective. Say you have realized that your team collaboration is much more efficient remotely, and as a team, you want to leverage it.

All three are possible, and the post-Covid-19 workplace may be the perfect testing ground for bending and shaping requests. If you are well prepared and understand how flexibility will impact your role productivity and that of your team, you are likely to succeed in these negotiations.

How to Ask Your Boss for a Flexible Work Arrangement

1. Understand your organization's policies (if they exist).

Review your firm's current policies around flexible work arrangements. Understand when and why your firm developed them. Identify the teams and employees who have made the most use of flexible work. Speak with trusted mentors and other team members to understand how flexibility may be linked to other employment issues such as compensation and benefits, performance evaluation, promotion, training, issues with compliance, law, etc. This understanding will allow you to know whether your ask will be seen as a bending or shaping request.

2. Understand your role and its relationship to those of your team members.

Think about the role interdependencies. Understand how your role fits with the roles of other members in your team. Talk to your team members about your shared responsibilities and learn about their preferred work schedules.

Divide the tasks into face to face and remote. Prepare a table summarizing the essential tasks that require face-to-face interactions and those that can be managed remotely. For all tasks that can be managed remotely, speak with your team members to identify what technology and tools will enable better remote collaboration. This will provide you with information on how your flexibility might influence both your and your team's role execution.

3. Document your successes with flexibility.

Create a file of evidence on how you have coordinated with your team and accomplished your goals working from home during the pandemic. Document your fluency in virtual collaboration.

For example, was there a project on the back burner that you fast-tracked while working from home because you were able to immerse yourself in the project and engage in strategic thinking? Examples like these build an evidence-based case and give you an opportunity to ask for specific equipment (tools and technology) to be more productive in your home office.

4. Have a plan B in place.

Think about the potential constraints and sticking points that your boss might bring up and resist your ask. Think about your boss's interests and concerns and the potential benefits of giving you flexibility. Consider presenting the flexibility ask as an experiment wherein you offer to engage in remote work for three or six months with regular reporting on your progress and an agreed-on definition of the performance criterion. By offering your boss more data and greater accountability, you are likely to lower the sense of risk.

• • •

Remember—your success at the negotiation table is determined by the mindset you have on what is and is not possible and how you do the groundwork and preparation before the conversation, rather than just how tough you are at the table. These steps will aid you in presenting a more durable case for your flexibility ask.

Adapted from "How to Negotiate Remote and Flexible Work Arrangements with Your Boss," on hbr.org ASCEND, June 9, 2020.

12

Returning to Work as a New Mother of Color

A conversation with Christine Michel Carter

Quick Takes

- New mothers of color frequently face impostor syndrome and additional challenges at work

- If you are a new mother of color, resist the urge to try to "fit in"

- Use your parental benefits—both for yourself and to benefit others

- Seek and support other mothers of color, especially through ERGs

- Connect with executives who are mothers

Christine Michel Carter is a subject matter expert on working parents and women's ERGs. She speaks frequently at conferences and corporate events on subjects such as maternal mental health, retaining women of color, and combating impostor syndrome. As a *ForbesWomen* senior contributor, she has written hundreds of articles aimed at helping and advocating for working parents. Christine has interviewed Vice President Kamala Harris on Black maternal health and has received a congressional citation for her work in ensuring that moms of color have access to vital information. And on top of raising her two school-age kids, she's the author of the novel *MOM AF* and the children's book *Can Mommy Go to Work?* HBR spoke with Christine in mid-2021 at a moment when the Covid-19 pandemic was receding in many parts of the world, but the wounds it had inflicted were still raw.

HBR: *Most of us are aware of the challenges new mothers face when they are returning to work, whether it's a lack of paid leave, workplace discrimination against parents, rigid schedules, or finding affordable, quality childcare.*

Do new mothers of color face additional challenges, and what are they?

CHRISTINE MICHEL CARTER: To start with, new mothers of color are more likely than their white peers to experience impostor syndrome—nagging doubts about their competence, even when they've been told otherwise. Impostor syndrome and racial discrimination work hand in hand to tear down their self-esteem and mental health, and this in turn affects their "ambient belonging"—a state of being comfortable in a space where they are feeling accepted, valued, and included. Ambient belonging is one of the social determinants of health: conditions in the places where people live, learn, work, and play that affect a wide range of health and quality-of-life risks and outcomes.

Another challenge is that mothers of color are relied on for care more heavily. Black women spend 12 more hours per week caring for children than white women do. They are more likely to live in multigenerational households and, according to LeanIn.Org, they spent nearly three times more hours per week caring for elderly or sick relatives during the pandemic. New mothers of color also are reporting themselves as receiving less frequent and lower-quality care; 44% of Black women reported not receiving any communication about Covid-19 from their provider, compared with 38% of white women.

HBR: *Like so many issues that are rooted in racism or unconscious bias, we can't put the onus of fixing culture just on these new mothers of color. Even so, we want these mothers to come back to work with the best mindset and plan they can. What tactics do you recommend new mothers of color should use to find success, as they measure it, in their first few months back to work?*

CC: Resist the urge to try and "fit in." We know that for minority professionals, finding success in corporate America often means significant compromise. On top of this, Black women also feel pressured to alter their voice, appearance, hair, and even personality daily in some corporate environments. In spite of this conforming, they are still paid lower wages than their white colleagues.

My advice: Bring your authentic self to work. You are a new mother with different needs, and those needs should be communicated to your employer. All too often, mothers are anxious about appearing uncommitted to their jobs, so they and other caregivers opt not to take advantage of employee benefits such as employee assistance programs, which offer solutions like therapy for employees or dependents or emergency childcare assistance. That leads employers to infer that moms and caregivers are managing fine at work, and then they don't feel the need to invest in caregiving benefits or, in some cases, even track data associated with caregiving employees.

The lack of compelling data leads to no changes in policy to support caregivers. Then what happens to mom and other caregivers? They feel unsupported by employers and struggle to keep up, and their declining performance leads to increased stigmas and biases against caregivers. This causes long-term change in organizational culture, and this is why it's so important for Black moms to bring their authentic selves and their needs to work.

HBR: *That's unconventional advice—that Black moms should play up their motherhood rather than downplay it. What kinds of outcomes do you see when new mothers truly own their motherhood in the workplace?*

CC: To me, it makes perfect sense: If companies want certain segments of their workforce to network, develop their talent, and bring diversity of thought to the organization, why wouldn't an employee express that they are in fact a member of that certain segment? I believe diversity is an inherent talent one can bring to the workforce. Also, Black moms playing up their motherhood is the only way unconscious biases toward Black women and working parents will be eliminated—change requires relentless authenticity and advocacy.

Reflecting personally on when I played up my motherhood at a tech startup, my relentless authenticity and advocacy involved researching the Fair Labor Standards

Act (FLSA) and the federal Break Time for Nursing Mothers law. I was the only Black mom (and mom and woman) in my office. Had I not owned my motherhood, I would have kept pumping in a bathroom stall. It also provided diversity of thought to the company. As their consumer marketer, I began thinking about our company's business model. I championed targeting a new consumer segment and revenue stream.

HBR: *That's an inspiring story! And wow—that is a lot of dimensions for you to be the "only" in your organization. Hopefully, most mothers of color can reach out to colleagues who share experiences similar to their own for support. What might that look like?*

CC: Mothers of color should seek support and best practices from one another. Employee resource groups (ERGs), which have been around for decades, exist at 90% of *Fortune* 500 companies. As a consultant, I've encouraged these ERGs to adopt not only formal mentorship programs, but informal opportunities for their members to build relationships as well. This lays the groundwork for support to happen: Employees uncover an even more personalized safe space. For example, when leadership within a women's ERG can identify and encourage engagement between members, the female employee feels not only directly supported by another woman, but indirectly supported by the organization.

HBR: *Let's look at the managerial side. What can individual managers do to make the situation better for their employees who are mothers of color? And how can these women work with their managers?*

CC: Recent data from the *State of Black Women in Corporate America* report by LeanIn.Org found that 59% of Black women have never had an informal interaction with a senior leader, compared with 47% of white women. And Black women self-reported that only one in three managers have checked in on them—defined as connecting privately with the employee to "check" their status, condition, or well-being. This is absolutely disheartening, especially when you consider this past year disproportionately affected these women. Simply checking in on Black mom professionals—exhibiting true empathy for your team members—is a welcome start. Employees are gauging right now whether their managers and their employers are treating them with respect and care.

HBR: *What about other allies in the workplace—colleagues, other parents? What can they do?*

CC: Other allies in the workplace should do the same, but let's be honest—most office culture breakdowns occur at the middle management level. Even in the midst of a pandemic, people aren't leaving companies; they're leaving bosses. Businesses need to train management on inclusive terminology and interrupting bias within micro-moments. Managers would do best to provide women with virtual support that meets them where they are and is available 24/7. They should help them identify and connect with executives in the organization who are mothers. They can be allies who have successfully climbed the corporate ladder and simultaneously juggled motherhood.

HBR: *What about from the organizational level? What actions should organizations, especially those that are committed to furthering diversity, inclusion, and belonging, be undertaking to make companies a better place for mothers who are women of color?*

CC: Outside of the table stakes like flexible work, speaker series, or career workshops, I'm often surprised at how many companies don't have a caregiving or working parents ERG. It's here they'd find best practices and understand how diverse the caregiving and working parents experience truly is. Adding such an ERG to inclusion objectives and key results would naturally make companies a better place for mothers who are women of color.

13

A First-Time Mom's Guide to Pumping Milk at Work

by Julia Beck and Courtney Cashman

Quick Takes

- Gather the supplies and tools you'll need
- Practice regularly before returning to work
- Understand what you're entitled to by law
- Learn the culture of your pumping room
- Set a schedule and stick to it
- Establish boundaries and communicate them to others

Kate is an executive who is both passionate about and masterful at her job. Throughout her pregnancy and after the birth of her first child, Kate was pleased to see that her office was an extremely warm, caring environment. When she returned after leave, she felt suitably prepared for pumping at work with support from a lactation consultant, a bounty of products, and an office with a door, which when locked would allow her to pump milk in private. Her colleagues and her boss were her biggest cheerleaders and made the experience one that Kate felt positive about.

Jessica, a physical therapist, had her first child in 2019. Her client base within a private physical therapy group was robust and loyal. She was able to coordinate with her organization's scheduling desk to allow time for two 30-minute pumping breaks per day. During these breaks, she would pump in her treatment room with the back of a chair wedged under the doorknob since there was no lock. Jessica's pay was based on the number of clients she saw, so her pumping breaks not only cut into her patient time, they also resulted in a drop in income.

Returning to work as a first-time mother is complex and challenging. And starting to pump at work puts you at the bottom of a steep learning curve. Every woman has a different experience. Whether yours is like Kate's, Jessica's, or somewhere in between, pumping at work involves a lot of difficult logistics and often stress.

The best strategies for finding success as a first-time pumping mother center around preparedness. It's critical to both understand the resources available to you and plan your time carefully. Here are a few tips to help you succeed in your goals, feel more supported, and reduce the stress that comes with pumping at work.

Prepare, plan, and plan again.

Your pumping plan begins before you even return to work. First, gather your supplies. The Affordable Care Act in the United States provides free pumps for all new mothers. If your budget permits, consider getting a second one to use at work so you don't need to lug it in each day. There are a broad range of goods that make pumping possible as well as comfortable (see the sidebar, "An Insider's Guide to Pumping Goods"). Don't skimp—pumping is tricky, and you will benefit from the best tools available. If you have access to a lactation consultant (check with your ob-gyn, medical insurer, and HR department before hiring one out of pocket), consider getting their advice to help pick the best products for you and create a plan for your return.

An Insider's Guide to Pumping Goods

Every new mother who has chosen to pump at work needs to start with a reliable electric pump and accessories that will help you pump efficiently. But there are additional tools that can make your sessions more convenient and pleasant.

- Hands-free equipment allows you to pump milk while leaving your fingers free to type or browse your device. Pumping bras are widely available, and some companies, such as Elvie, also make hands-free pumps.

- Use microwavable sanitation bags to clean parts with ease without the need for a sink and soap. Ameda makes the largest bags on the market for simple transport.

- Leaking and nipple pain happen. Be sure to have high-quality reusable nipple pads (consider

Then, spend time getting used to your pump regularly at least two weeks before returning to work. Learning to pump, understanding the accessories, cleaning and storing parts, timing your sessions, and other nuances can be a lot to process. "Logistics are not intuitive," shares

Dr. Brown's) to absorb unexpected drips and a healing nipple cream for any discomfort. Lansinoh, a lansinol-based formula, or Bamboobies, which is coconut oil–based, are excellent.

- A big water bottle, healthy snacks, and lip balm are essential. Use them throughout the day, but also have them handy when you pump (though it's worth checking if your lactation room allows food first).

- Have an extra bra and shirt in case of leakage or spills, though an all-purpose scarf is also a great alternative.

- Be prepared for highs and lows. Lansinoh TheraPearl pads are useful to manage clogged ducts when cooled, support milk letdown when hot, and ease the process of weaning when you are ready.

nurse and lactation consultant Torrey Potter. "A few (not so dry) runs are quite wise." Practice both to get the hang of pumping and to build a freezer stash of milk (after all, your child will need something to eat on your first day back). Get an idea of what kind of producer you are, and don't be hard on yourself if you aren't producing as much as you hoped. People have high and often unreasonable expectations of how things will go. Be patient.

Understand what you're entitled to.

Every country has its own laws and regulations about what working mothers are entitled to when it comes to pumping. In the United States, the Affordable Care Act requires employers to provide "reasonable break time for an employee to express breast milk for her nursing child for 1 year after the child's birth each time such employee has need to express the milk," and they must provide "a place, other than a bathroom, that is shielded from view and free from intrusion from coworkers and the public, which may be used by an employee to express breast milk." Start by understanding your national laws, and then move on to what is guaranteed at the local level.

Talk to your HR department to find out where the dedicated pumping spaces are in your building and if there are any benefits you're entitled to as a new mother. Some companies, for instance, may have call-in access to nurses, doulas, or lactation consultants who can provide advice or support as you return to work.

Learn the culture.

The protocols of using pumping rooms can vary across organizations. Some companies require online registration and scheduling, while others ask for a simple knock on the door to see if it's occupied. Find out in advance what you need to do so you're not surprised (and bursting) on your first day back.

Take a close look at the room and you'll learn more. What supplies are provided—and what do you need to do to make sure it's a comfortable space for others who may share the room with you? Some rooms may provide anything from a hospital-grade pump, a refrigerator, and a sink, while others keep only a chair near an electrical socket. If it's a shared space, can you leave pumping supplies in the room or are lockers provided? How are people marking their supplies and milk? Are there sanitary wipes or other cleaning supplies? Support the other pumping mothers in your organization by leaving the room as neat or neater than when you first arrived. Everyone wants a hygienic space to pump.

Establish your timetable.

Potter advises, "If you want to keep our milk supply up, you will need to build and keep a routine." Determine how many times a day you need to pump and for how long. Everyone's requirements are different based on their child's needs and feeding habits, so look at what works best for you.

Also consider how long each session needs to be. Don't just think about the 15 or so minutes you'll be actively pumping. Reserve time for setup and cleanup. Untangling tubing, labeling bottles and milk bags, and wiping down surfaces might seem like quick tasks, but they add up.

Set boundaries—and communicate them.

Put your pumping times into your work calendar. By marking these periods as scheduled, you'll ensure that others won't double-book you. You're also signaling to yourself that these are important appointments for you to keep.

It's also necessary to establish boundaries with others. While pumping may be top-of-mind for you, your co-workers might not think about it until they see you walk by with a pump and a cooler. Since you've put pumping times on your calendar—even if they're just labeled "reserved"—you've already taken the first step to ensuring they respect this time. But there will be instances when you will need to push back in the moment. Competing meetings pop up and conversations run long, so be prepared to excuse yourself using whatever form of communication you're most comfortable with, whether it's openly saying, "I can't. I have to go pump" or a simple "I have a hard stop at 1:00." Explain if you can't accommodate a virtual meeting or call due to pumping: "I won't be able to join at this time, even with my video off." Even if your colleagues are aware of your commitment to pumping at work, they won't know that you need to pump *now* unless you communicate your boundaries. Whatever you do, don't skip—missed pumping sessions can result in lower milk supply, discomfort, blocked ducts, or even mastitis.

Find support.

At times you may feel alone in your pumping journey, but you are joining a society of many. Seek out other mothers with children a few months to a few years older than yours and talk to them about their experiences. These women can share best practices from where to store supplies to the complex realities of business travel, including best times to fly, how to arrange for milk shipment, in-hotel storage, and pumping at conferences.

Consider, too, alternative sources of support. External peer support groups can help with anything from logistical tips to emotional support, especially when it comes to working-mom guilt. Lactation consultants and other experts can also help learn how to pump more effectively, establish goals, and overcome specific challenges. And don't forget the power of your friends and family. Your village is a powerful provider of what you don't yet know.

Be flexible.

Pumping at work is a learning curve—and it's not set in stone. Over time, you might need to adjust your schedule because another teammate might need the room at the same time or you need to add another session because you're producing less milk than anticipated (or your baby is drinking more). You may have days where you can work easily while pumping using hands-free pumping supplies; other times, you need to focus on the task. Be kind to yourself. Some days will seem more challenging than others. Be willing to adjust as necessary.

● ● ●

You will be hard-pressed to find a first-time pumping mother who does not have a horror story or two to share about workplace pumping (the accidental walk-in by a coworker or spilling that "liquid gold"). But most of them agree that it was worth the effort in the end. Side-step stress by practicing and preparing, knowing what you're entitled to, and carefully planning and protecting your time. There is no perfect way pump at work, but you can find what works for you.

Adapted from "A New Mother's Guide to Pumping at Work," on hbr.org, August 6, 2021 (product #H06IL3).

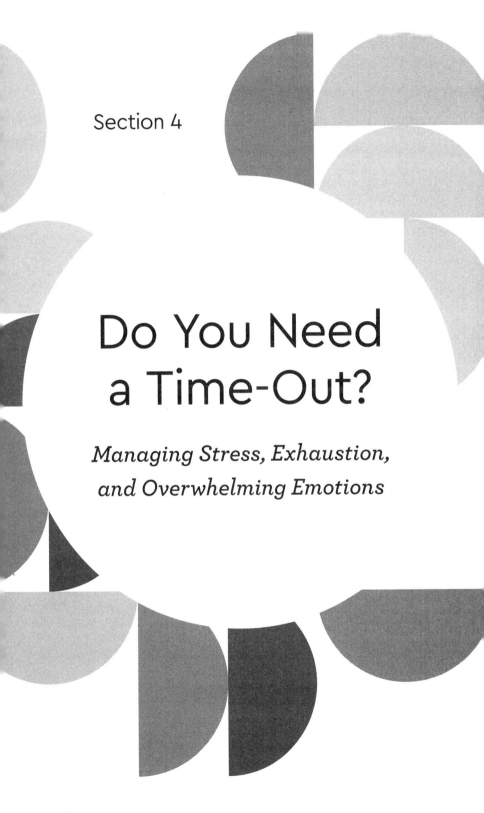

Section 4

Do You Need a Time-Out?

Managing Stress, Exhaustion, and Overwhelming Emotions

How You Can Prioritize Sleep

by Amie M. Gordon and Christopher M. Barnes

Quick Takes

- Set a consistent sleep routine—and stick to it
- Limit blue light and keep screens out of your bedroom
- Avoid talking about serious matters before bed
- Make the most of your family's sleeping schedules
- Shape your work schedule around your family
- Don't stress about a bad night's sleep

When you're juggling a job, kids, and all the details of everyday life, sleep feels like a luxury you can afford later, when your kids are grown. Instead of sleeping, parents use those precious few moments they have at the end of the day to catch up on work or take some much-needed me-time. But the problems that come with not getting enough sleep won't simply step aside and wait until retirement. Sleep deprivation magnifies the challenges in an already difficult life. One area where sleep deprivation takes its toll is on our relationships, both at home and in the workplace.

Research from across the globe has linked general sleep tendencies with relationship quality, showing that people who sleep worse experience less satisfying relationships, particularly with romantic partners.[1] People are more likely to fight with their partners after a poor night of sleep, and couples have more difficulty resolving conflicts if *either* partner slept badly the night before. The effects go the other way as well—people tend to sleep worse after fighting with their romantic partners. This creates the possibility of a vicious cycle in which poor sleep begets conflict, and conflict begets poor sleep.

Additionally, research suggests that children who are exposed to more marital conflict tend to sleep worse, which may have further negative effects on the parents' sleep. In contrast, children whose parents have higher-quality relationships tend to sleep better.[2]

Sleep also plays a role in how we relate to our children. One study found that mothers who had more disrupted sleep were less sensitive to their 18-week-old infants than those who had more continuous sleep. Good sleep may also be a protective factor; both parents and children who sleep better are more resilient in the face of stressors.[3] Overall, getting the sleep we need helps us have better relationships with our children.

Although our sleep tends to happen at home, we bring the consequences of poor sleep into the workplace, too. Leaders who report sleeping worse tend to engage in more abusive behaviors toward their employees (such as yelling at them in front of their colleagues) and have damaged relationships with those employees. Sleep-deprived leaders are also less charismatic and generally less effective in their leadership roles. Research indicates that overall, businesses benefit when employees are well rested.[4]

Deprioritizing sleep is one way to deal with the heavy demands on a working parent's limited time, but the consequences are clear: Both at home and in the workplace, relationships are worse when people don't prioritize their sleep.

So, what is a time-famished working parent to do?

Since physicists have yet to unlock the secrets to freezing time, working parents must turn to more feasible means to get a good night's sleep. Here are a few evidence-based tips to help working parents take care of themselves and create good sleeping practices when it seems like there is no time to do so. Getting good sleep won't give you more time, but it will help you make better use of the time you have.

Make sleep a priority.

Recognize that your days will feel more productive if you get enough sleep, which can give you a sense of having more time. There's always the desire to fit in "one last thing" or put off going to sleep, but a good night of sleep will give you much-needed resources to deal with the demands of daily life. Figure out how much sleep you need to feel well rested (the recommendation in the United States is seven to nine hours for adults). Decide what time you need to wake up in the morning, then count backward. Set a bedtime alarm, giving yourself an extra 30 minutes to an hour to unwind and get ready for bed each night. Creating a relaxing bedtime routine for the whole family (dim lights, relaxing music, stories in bed) might be one way to get everyone to wind down together.

Set a consistent sleep routine for yourself and your children.

One of the best ways to sleep well is to have a consistent sleep routine. This tells your body when to wake up and when to go to sleep so that it releases melatonin at the right time, making it easier to fall asleep and stay asleep. A consistent routine won't just get you more sleep; it will get you more high-quality sleep. Keep this routine on both the days you're working and the days you're not. Although it is enticing, using the weekends to do a major "catch-up" on sleep is actually counterproductive. Sleeping in late will feel good that day, but it throws off your body clock and fails to address the larger issue of having a consistent schedule that allows enough time for sleep on a daily basis. Children of all ages get more sleep when parents help structure the child's sleep schedule.

Limit exposure to blue light at night.

Blue light tells your body it's daytime, which can mess with your sleep. Smartphones, computers, and tablets emit this blue light. To prevent this, use blue-light filters (built into most tablets and smartphones) or wear blue-light-blocking glasses when using a screen in the hours leading up to your bedtime routine. On the other hand, exposure to bright blue light in the morning is a great way to start your day. Exposure to bright light when you first wake up helps set your circadian rhythm and lets your body know it's time to be alert.

Keep screens out of your bedroom.

In an ever-connected world, working parents may want to check their email one last time or scroll through Twitter for a few minutes after they're in bed. But a big part of good sleep hygiene is giving your body a chance to unwind before you fall asleep. We also tend to lack self-regulation the more tired we get, so while you might only intend to go online for a few minutes, those handful of minutes can quickly turn into an hour or more. Leave your screens outside the room—or put them in airplane mode before you get in bed.

Quit while you're ahead.

We've all wanted to stay up just a little longer to finish the task we're working on. But if you're trying to work when it's time to go to bed, you're going to be more inefficient and make more mistakes. Instead, stick to your bedtime and return to your task the next day when you'll be refreshed, thinking clearly, and can get it done in half the time.

Don't stress about those inevitable nights of poor sleep.

While a consistent sleep routine is great, everyone experiences poor sleep at some point. Worrying about your sleep can become a problem of its own. Instead, recognize that your body is resilient and can handle short-term sleep problems and find ways to de-stress before bed to help you relax and sleep well.

Beyond ways to make your sleep more consistent and habitual, consider these relationship-based strategies to prevent the inevitable conflicts that can arise out of lack of sleep:

Don't start talking about serious matters right before bed.

Although you've likely been told to never go to bed angry, a good night of sleep might also help you deal more constructively with conflict. If you can, save serious matters for a time when you're both awake and have the energy to talk. This may seem impossible, but like sleep, building in time to talk when you aren't tired can help the rest of your relationship run more smoothly. You can apply this to your workplace as well—don't wait until the end of the day when you're worn out to deal with difficult conversations or important brainstorming sessions.

Give your family and colleagues the benefit of the doubt.

The people in your life are likely just as tired as you are, so if your partner forgets to call you on their way home from work, assume it's because they had a difficult workday and not because they don't value your time. If your child is only giving one-word answers at dinner, remind yourself they may just be exhausted from an active day at school and not uninterested in what you have to say. And when your colleague forgets to confirm a meeting, check to see how they're doing personally before writing them off as unreliable.

Work together as efficiently as possible to reduce decision fatigue and inefficiency.

Have explicit conversations at home about household and childcare duties so that everyone is on the same page. Create a shared grocery list online so that anyone can add items to it. Create and share calendars so that you don't have to have a big discussion each time one of you is trying to schedule a task. Reducing unnecessary work can help free up time for the things you really need, like sleep.

If you and your partner have different sleeping times, make the most of it.

Having a different bedtime from your partner might seem problematic when your schedules don't overlap—whether those differences are due to personal preferences or work schedules. However, you may be able to leverage this difference by putting the person who wakes up early in charge of the morning routine and the night owl in charge of bedtime.

Buy time where you can.

If you can afford it, buy yourself time to sleep by paying other people to do some of your work for you, like housecleaning or grocery delivery. Research indicates that people who buy time tend to be happier.

Look into the possibility of flextime.

If your job allows it, being able to work from home or shape your work schedule around your family might help you feel less stressed and sleep better. For example, if you're an early riser, you might benefit from working at home in the morning before your family gets up and adjusting your hours accordingly. Consider being flexible with your family time as well. For instance, some families with full schedules might find that breakfast together works better than the traditional family dinner, so you can devote those evening hours to spending more time with the baby, cementing a toddler's bedtime routine, or unwinding after a long day, without the added stress of meal prep.

• • •

When you feel like you have no time to sleep is exactly when you need sleep the most. Finding a way to prioritize consistent, high-quality sleep can help you better navigate the demands of your everyday life, from better interactions with your family to better sleep for your children to better relationships at work.

Adapted from "How Working Parents Can Prioritize Sleep," on hbr.org, March 31, 2020 (product #H05HR7).

Don't Let PPD Undermine Your Return to Work

by Julia Beck

Quick Takes

- The transition back to work is a risk factor for post-partum depression

- Therapy, medication, and support are the best ways to lessen and overcome PPD

- Call on your village, and supplement it with additional services

- Embrace and accept that it's normal to struggle as a new parent

- Avoid unrealistic depictions of new parenthood

- Return to work gradually, and be prepared to adjust if your plan isn't working

Sarah was well versed at the fine art of excelling. She was a Division 1 collegiate soccer player, and upon graduation, she transitioned with her signature ease into the highly competitive corporate world, working for a well-respected global IT company as their North American events leader. Moving with the same athletic grace from entry-level planner to senior manager within five years, Sarah was already well-known in the organization for tending to urgently needed adjustments in real time. In August 2018, she was excited to learn she was pregnant. The next spring, Sarah and her husband welcomed a baby girl named Ameilia Jeanne, or AJ for short.

While AJ was well and thriving, Sarah's time on leave was full of complicated transitions. She and her husband had decided to move from San Antonio to Austin for his new job, and in the new city she felt lost, with little comfort or connection. Even so, she was sure that her return to work after a three-month parental leave would bring her back to feeling like herself—successful and in control.

Going back to work the following August, Sarah plunged back into a full schedule. But things weren't the same. While managing a large, complicated trade show in Las Vegas, a three-hour flight away from her family, she found herself in an unfamiliar place: She felt like she had no idea what she was doing. Her travel schedule cut time she spent with her daughter to 45 minutes a day on average. Agents at TSA security checkpoints ruined her breast milk and harassed her about being away from her baby in the first place. She found herself sinking into distress and overwhelmed by thoughts of failure. She became sleep deprived and came down with perioral dermatitis. Eventually, she experienced a range of suicidal thoughts, which she kept hidden from her support system, including her husband. Sarah was suffering from severe postpartum depression (PPD).

While PPD is physiological in origin, for Sarah it was exacerbated by her failure to find her professional footing. She clung to work desperately as a means to feel stable again, yet she continued to plummet. In time, her ability to function in all aspects of her life decreased. Six months after returning from leave, Sarah left her job, an outcome that had been unthinkable a year before. Throughout it all, she hid her PPD from her boss and colleagues. Many were surprised to hear she was struggling. Talking about it would have felt like displaying vulnerability in a way that was impossible in her unsupportive work environment. "I thought of myself as disciplined, strong, and mentally capable, but after this, I realized that PPD does not discriminate." Sarah wishes she had known more before she fell so far.

More people are starting to know the basics of PPD, and how common it is in the weeks after birth. Most people *don't* know that PPD can strike up to a year after birth—long after most maternity leaves are finished—and that the stress of returning to work is a risk factor for exacerbating PPD. You (or your partner) are not likely to experience PPD as extreme as Sarah's, but failing to understand its risks and realities before and during return to work can be dangerous to your well-being and your career. This chapter will help you understand some small steps you can take to lower your risk and return to work with confidence.

PPD and Work: What You Need to Know

The facts are simply this: As a new mother, you are not the same woman you were prior to giving birth—not physically, not emotionally, and certainly not in terms of responsibilities.

For many, the months leading up to childbirth can be exhausting and filled with anxiety, but from belly kicks to showers to babymoons, at the same time, this is often a period of anticipation, celebration, and togetherness. Contrast that to the situation of newly minted mothers, who are often home alone with a new baby, recovering both physically and emotionally from birth while attempting to make sense of their new roles. Mixed with rapid hormone shifts, this isolation can act as a trigger for a spectrum of postpartum mood disorders, ranging from "baby blues" to postpartum depression to postpartum psychosis (a severe form of PPD, which Sarah experienced). (The Mayo Clinic does an excellent job of outlining specific symptoms.[1])

Meanwhile, another sudden drop-off occurs with maternal health care and support. Washington, DC–based ob-gyn Dr. Lauren Messinger says, "We develop such strong relationships with women over the course of prenatal care, ultimately seeing them every week; then after delivery, we now go six weeks without so much as a scheduled call or visit." Dr. Messinger's office has now added two-week postpartum visits.

And going back to work increases the stress. Even with the most powerful and genuine peer support, return is a shock. Instead of fitting comfortably into your old place, you find yourself in a new job, as a new person. The one area in which you reliably thrived and led the pack is now a steep upward climb, with a learning curve to match. Simply starting and ending your workday, which once required little thought, may become an ordeal as you juggle complicated new logistics, hormones, and exhaustion. This was the case with Sarah—already struggling during leave, she thought her return to work would be a cure-all. In fact, it was the final straw.

How to Best Prepare for Your Return

Fortunately, these feelings are all normal and can be addressed successfully. As Ann Smith, founder of Post-partum Support International, points out: "PPD is the number one complication of childbearing. While 14% of women suffer, it is treatable. PPD is managed through a three-legged approach that combines therapy, medication, and peer support." While there is no surefire or one-size-fits-all solution to managing the very personal challenges of PPD, the following methods will help you create a sense of confidence as a first-time working parent and serve as a reminder that despite the challenge of the moment, this too shall pass.

Call on your village—and supplement it with additional support.

Surrounding yourself with loving, experienced friends, family, and caregivers is essential—not just in the first few weeks, but throughout your parental leave. One way to go further is hiring a postpartum doula. Twenty-one states offer up to $1,500 reimbursement for doula services. Take advantage of this hands-on opportunity to build confidence and skills. There is no better way to understand the new roles, learn best practices, and—most important—the pace of new parenting. The help is not only for you to learn skills such as how to swaddle or bathe your child but also to offer perspective and kindness to yourself. Those who have already been there know this and will nurture you as you nurture your baby.

Embrace who you are.

"Some women simply are not great newborn mothers," says Smith. Others find motherhood a new calling and start rethinking their careers during leave. Still others don't really hit their stride as parents until their kids reach the school years. All of these reactions are normal. In fact, honesty, even pride around your strengths and weaknesses, will create a healthier path for any new parent, especially a first-time parent.

Say "so long" to social media.

Warning: New motherhood is not as it appears on Instagram. Limit your exposure. Give yourself the chance to feel confident and secure on your own terms. Unrealistic social media images lead to negative self-views and insecurity, opening the door to PPD-related challenges. Smith shares, "We have a cultural issue—the idea that a real mother should not need help or assistance—and social media has made a mess of expectations that real moms do it all. This is not realistic and, in fact, dangerous." She urges caution with online support as well.

"Nonprofessional online support groups can prove to be even more of a hazard—the words, 'You've got this, mama' can cause a woman suffering from the insecurities and anxieties of PPD to feel like even more of a failure."

Reclaim sleep.

Sleep deprivation as the parent of a newborn is a given, but it's still problematic. Sleep provides energy, increases milk supply, and keeps a new mother feeling capable as opposed to vulnerable and insecure. Ask for and accept help from your village—they want to help you find sleep. There are professional options as well. Services like Let Mommy Sleep work with parents to provide the opportunity to sleep and recharge. Founder Denise Stern is careful with placing very specific caregivers in the home of first-time parents. "Finding the right fit for first-time parents is essential, [someone] who is interested in caring for mother and child as both adjust."

Connect through education and meditation.

Self-knowledge and connection to yourself encourage your sense of security. Expectful has an app that facilitates meditation and hosts courses such as "Back to Business—Finding Your Work-Life Balance as a Working Mother." The Breastfeeding Center of Greater Washington offers group classes including a range specific to navigating postpartum stresses—check in with your ob-gyn, the hospital where you gave birth, or other mothers to find classes in your area. Research and choose your options prenatally. Find the right fit in terms of chemistry and personality. The power of connecting with others deep in similar experiences along with a well-trained leader is an essential tool for empowerment and feeling less isolation or, worse, failure.

Be ready.

All of the resources and care available for first-time mothers mentioned in this piece should be as well researched as the right stroller or babysitter and accessible when you need them. Start today, whether you're expecting, on leave, or already back to work. These supports may be covered by your medical insurance or as an employee benefit. Ask your ob-gyn and your HR department. Know these providers' contact info, rates, and rules of engagement. Another surprise or a panicked search for a care provider will only worsen things. Be prepared for a search: There is a high level of need, and regulated support is meager.

Return gradually—and know when it's not working.

Sarah made the mistakes of ramping up too quickly, then suffering in silence. Options for creating a smoother return include remote work, gradual return, and peer mentoring to ease the transition. Even for the those who are well prepared, there are no promises or guarantees. You may find that you are simply not ready to take on the pressures of returning to work—or at least *not yet*. Work with your employer to understand your options. Know that they want you to bring your best version of yourself back to work also.

• • •

Sarah ultimately sought out professional help. It took time, but she was dedicated to improvement, and she recovered personally and professionally. She started her own business, which was not only a good match for her lifestyle but also thrived as a result of the Covid-19 pandemic. She has found professional and personal relationships that are better suited for her needs. There simply is no one-size-fits-all approach to addressing the spectrum of PPD. Investments in your own postpartum physical and mental health are investments in both your career and your well-being as a new mother and as a woman.

Everyday Joys

A conversation with Amy Jen Su and Kevin Evers

Quick Takes

- Find self-compassion when you feel unsuccessful as a parent or a worker
- We all have moments where feel more reactive and less effective
- Learn to notice these moments and compassionately bring yourself back
- Use small rituals to keep yourself centered

---

efore I had kids, I knew that becoming a parent would be the hardest thing I would ever do. But I was OK with that. Why? Because I thought I'd feel far more joy than anguish. Sadly, that wasn't the case.

To be honest, I rarely felt joy my first two years as a dad. My daughter, Maisie, suffered from colic and acid reflux and had a general bad attitude about sleep. On good days, she was extremely irritable. On bad days, she was downright inconsolable. One time on a six-hour car ride, she screamed the entire time. And this wasn't an anomaly. This was our life.

I couldn't believe it. Everyone had told me that this would be the most joyful period of my life. Instead, it felt like the worst. I was exhausted, rattled, depressed. At home, I felt like a five-alarm fire. At work, I felt like a zombie.

I don't remember much from that time. The birthdays, the first steps, the first word. But I do remember my little girl, her face as red as a boiled Maine lobster, screaming for my help. Everything else is hazy.

That's why when my son, Willie, was born, I vowed to cherish every sound, every smile, and every gesture. I wanted to reclaim what I had lost. I've had my moments. Sometimes I've been able to be totally present. Pausing and savoring the little things. I love how Willie bursts out laughing whenever he makes a mistake, like falling or getting his arm stuck in his shirt. I try to do the same with Maisie, paying particular attention when she speaks.

When I'm in this hyperaware mode, when I'm trying to cultivate joy, I'm more playful and present and thankful. I'm much happier. But it's not easy to sustain.

My kids have taught me that joy is a job, that it's up to me to find it and savor it. I've been trying really hard. I owe it to them and I owe it to myself, but it's a struggle.

Obviously, I could use some help, so I invited leadership development coach Amy Jen Su, who helps clients step up their endurance and effectiveness at work.

KEVIN EVERS: *Amy, the biggest problem that you explained in your book* The Leader You Want to Be *is one I have been facing ever since I've become a working parent: I rarely feel like the person I want to be. I rarely feel like the worker I want to be. I rarely feel like the parent I want to be. As I was reading through your book, I found a lot of kindred spirits. On the very first page, you have this great contrast between Leader A and Leader B. Could you describe that?*

AMY JEN SU: Sure, Kevin. Leader A and Leader B in some ways is all of us. We all have a Leader A part of ourselves. This is when we're able to meet the moment we're in with a little more openness—a wider, broader perspective—and somehow we're swimming with the current and we feel a little more ease and effectiveness.

Conversely, we all have a Leader B response to life as well. It's almost like when you know you woke up on the wrong side of the bed. Your view of life feels narrower; everything happening feels a little more personal; and we end up more reactive, more overwhelmed, more stressed. And so the whole idea of Leader A and Leader B was when to say, "Hey, you're not in it alone." We all have these responses to life, A and B, and that heuristic and that language were really created just to give you a chance to say, "How do I notice this and how do I, with more compassion, bring myself gently back to A?"

KE: *Before I was a working parent, I felt like I was in Leader A mode most of the time. Then I became a working parent, and the stress levels were just off the charts. I had so much going on and I had this beautiful little baby, yet it was really hard to feel joy in the moments. At work, I felt like I was turbocharged. I was striving more than I ever had before. Before I was very much into what was giving me purpose, what was giving me meaning, but then with this baby, I felt this urge to provide for her, and I think I overdid it—"I need to get promoted, I need to keep moving up in my career"—and I lost focus on what was really important.*

AS: A life change like having a child brings with it a complete change in our bandwidth and our capacity—I know, I have a 15-year-old now. Suddenly your baby is born and there really are not enough hours in the day. The "shoulds" in our mind just get louder and louder. Suddenly becoming a parent brings the full paradox and wide range of human emotion: "How is it that with this joyful, wonderful being in my life, I'm also more stressed, more frantic, more upset than I've ever been?" Realizing you're not alone in holding these feelings is so important.

KE: *I feel that as working parents it's really difficult and we're going to have B days. That's why I love the dynamic between Leader A and Leader B, because we should strive for a state of Leader A, but it's not something that we'll necessarily feel every minute of the day. I felt a lot of self-compassion reading your book. What are some of the obstacles that get in our way from feeling like we're Leader A most of the time?*

AS: One of them is just time. We're trying to fit in all the things we hope to do both as a parent and as a professional. Suddenly we're not only accountable and responsible in our jobs—we feel this whole new weight of accountability as a parent in wanting to provide and in wanting to be there. Trying to be Leader A 100% of the time is expecting ourselves to be superhuman, and that's not the intent at all. When I've been out in the field talking to professionals, the highest number I ever heard from anyone was 60/40 ratio. I think the question isn't, "How do I be Leader A all the time?"; it's really "What's my center of gravity, A or B? What's my response to life, A or B? And can I notice when I'm slipping into B mode? And can I bring myself back compassionately?"

KE: *Sometimes if I'm not careful, I tend to slip into B mode and I don't even realize it. And it can last days or weeks, and in some cases it can last months. I'm like a fish in water. I need sort of mental tricks and things to make sure that I don't fall into that trap.*

AS: Yeah, I think that slippery slope between A and B exists for all of us. We're all vulnerable to it. As you mentioned, try to notice the cues for when you're shifting. For me, when I start reaching into the pantry a lot, and I find myself every hour saying, "I deserve a candy bar or a bag of chips," I'm just trying to find a way to cope. I am starting to slip into B mode. Knowing your own cues is a really important piece of this.

KE: *My wife and I have designed a cue with each other to notice when we're in B mode. A lot of that has to do with a lack of sleep. One of us will start ranting, or we'll just get down that slippery slope of negativity, and we'll just say to each other, "We're just tired." And it's like a splash of water*

*to the face. You're like, "Oh, OK. I'm in B mode right now.
What can I do to get out of that mode?"*

AS: I love the just naming what's actually going on: "I'm
tired." "We're not getting enough sleep." And acknowl-
edging that can often be that moment of wakeup call of
"Wow, let's now have a dialogue around, how do we take
turns? Who gets to fill up their gas tank tonight, and
then I'll trade you the next night?"

KE: *You talk about presence and pause a lot in your book.
And I feel like those two things are really important to
cultivate and feel joy. I know these are hard to achieve,
especially as a working parent, but do you have any advice on how to create more awareness and more pause in
our lives?*

AS: They go hand in hand. First, it's just the awareness
of the importance of it. Second, rituals are so important in life. It doesn't need to be 45 minutes of going to
a yoga class. It can be as simple as giving yourself daily
permission to transition from work to home. I think we
just need to have that moment of *"OK, I'm about to transition from work to home. I need to give myself permission
to close the laptop lid."* And sometimes that's just taking
five minutes to get recentered, sitting in the chair, taking
a breath. I'm a big fan of breathing techniques that are

quick and fast. If we take a breath in for four counts and we hold that for seven, and then we exhale for eight, it's amazing how two rounds of breath work can bring our mind, heart, and body back together.

KE: *Do you have any parting advice for someone like me who feels like they're in Leader B mode more than Leader A mode?*

AS: I would just say, Kevin, that I feel great comfort that I'm right there with you. I've been coaching for a long time and certainly don't have all the answers, and a lot of the book was actually my sorting out and trying to come to peace with the fact that A and B is probably just a life condition. We're going to be moving in and out of both those states. But we can be a little kinder to ourselves.

Adapted from "Family Management: Everyday Joys" on Women at Work *(podcast), April 12, 2021.*

Today Plus 20 Years

*Your Career Ahead
as a Working Parent*

17

Ramp Up Your Career After Parental Leave

by Lisa Quest

Quick Takes

- Identify your career goals
- Cut out tasks and meetings that don't advance your goals
- Focus on what you can do in the time you have
- Conduct regular conversations at work and at home
- Reassess your goals and adjust course
- Pay it forward

Returning from parental leave can be a jarring inflection point that too often results in people curtailing their responsibilities or leaving their jobs altogether. While many women choose to return to work after maternity leave, many others find that it's not sustainable and leave or take on reduced roles. Seventeen percent of women and 4% of men stop working in the five years following childbirth, according to research recently conducted at the Universities of Bristol and Essex in the United Kingdom.[1] Harvard economist Claudia Goldin has found that the gender wage gap in America is the largest for women in their prime childbearing years.[2]

Navigating a system that was not designed for career paths that balance work with family can easily feel like a mission-practically-impossible even in the best of times. And when the job market is weak, many people will become even more pessimistic about the possibility of persuading an employer to accept a flexible work arrangement.

After two maternity leaves, I've discovered that some companies are willing to let people redesign their positions in a way that will allow them not just to continue their careers, but to accelerate them. It means setting clear goals, forensically analyzing how you spend your time, consciously not doing things that aren't core to meeting your goals, overcommunicating, and then course correcting when required.

Set Clear Goals

In order for any corporate machinery to try to accommodate your career goals, you first need to identify them. If you're not sure what your dreams are, no one can help you realize them. So step back and ask yourself: What do I *really* want?

What are your immediate objectives after you return from your parental leave? What are your long-term goals? Do you want to run your company one day? Or do you want to slow down your career and focus on your family? Or do you hope for some combination of both? All of these options can work—as long as you're honest with yourself and your employer.

If you can't articulate your answers, a parental leave is a great time to reflect on them. Being up with a tiny human at 3 a.m. can give you some time for self-reflection. In my case, it was difficult to envision my long-term goals and to figure out how to achieve them until I took a break from the daily grind on my maternity leaves. During my first leave, I resolved that I wanted to continue in consulting, a field with predominantly male leadership, as a partner at the consulting firm Oliver Wyman. But I also wanted to leave work every day at 6 p.m. to spend time with my family, and I wanted to take August off to travel from my base in London to visit family in Canada.

During my second leave, I decided that I hoped to play a major role in building out our firm's public-sector practice and lead our anti–financial crime business, where I would interact widely and often at the highest levels of our firm, overseeing multiple project teams in multiple countries at any given time. But I also wanted to be able to prioritize my family whenever I needed to. I adjusted my schedule accordingly, so now, instead of leaving work at 6 p.m. every day, I might take off one Monday per month. If I have an emergency doctor's appointment for my child, or if any of a potential million other things crop up unexpectedly with my family life, I can drop work if I need to or I can comfortably agree with my partner that he will handle the situation. In turn, if I have to work in the evening, I don't let it stress me out.

Forensically Analyze How You Spend Your Time

After you've identified your goals, forensically analyze how you spend your time at work and cut out anything that's not aligned with your objectives. Before you go on maternity leave, be clear about what you're working on, whom you're working with, and how you intend to rejoin your team. That way, once you return, you can more easily delegate or drop anything that does not speed up progress.

For people who already work fairly autonomously, this is generally straightforward. But if you are in a more senior position, you'll likely have to say no more often to supporting projects and corporate initiatives that are not directly related to your ambitions. This can be tricky, since there's a risk of being perceived as less committed to your company if you turn down extra work. Still, you must: If you take on too much, you may underdeliver on your work or family commitments, or both. Discuss the right balance with coworkers. People will generally understand if you make it crystal clear how you will still contribute on a broader level, but in a deliberate and agreed-on way by focusing on your goals.

Concentrate on what you *can* do within the time you have and excel at that. When I returned to work following my second maternity leave, I gave up supporting a major part of our business to focus purely on building out our economic crime advisory work with the public sector. Narrowing my focus in this way allowed me to devote the time necessary to develop much more insightful content in my specific area. As a result, we've been able to support the most sophisticated financial centers in improving their financial crime defenses. I miss supporting the other part of our business. But I would make the same decision again.

Overcommunicate

Overcommunicate your aspirations with your employer, colleagues, and family openly and honestly. Share a detailed parental leave plan with your boss that lays out what you want to achieve and the clients and areas that you want to cover. Schedule meetings with your boss before you leave, about a month before you come back, and monthly afterward to discuss how things are going. That way, they can step in to offer support when needed.

It's also important to have continual conversations with your partner at home. Persistently check on how your balance of work and home life is going. In my house, this changes every week. We constantly talk—or frantically text in the middle of the day—about who will pick up our oldest from day care and who can travel on which dates.

Course Correct

Be prepared to adjust. It's impossible to know what it's like to juggle your family and your career until you're in the thick of it. So be open to reassessing your goals and course correct as required.

You may find that you can do more than you expected. When I first came back from maternity leave, I was convinced that I wouldn't be able to commit to multiple client-facing roles. But once I set boundaries and became better at delegating, I found I had more time in my day than anticipated and could gradually take on more.

But accept that things will also not always work out as you'd hoped. I had to take a step back from one global initiative because the team, spread out across multiple time zones, would meet exactly at the time that I wanted to be home with my boys. After sleepless teething nights, I've lost four—yes, four—passports and misplaced countless bank cards and travel coffee cups. At times, our kitchen looks like it was hit by a tornado after we rush out the door in the morning. Don't let these kinds of mishaps cause stress—smile and realize that you're doing the best you can.

Be open and honest when your best-laid plans go awry. That way, the broader team can understand that it is not always an easy journey.

Be a Champion for Others

By bringing your whole self to work, you can encourage your employer to think through, and overcome, the potential obstacles involved in supporting not just your own flexible work arrangements, but also those of others. Actively and visibly support people in a similar position. Support individuals when the risks they have taken have failed and remind the organization, and the individual, that taking risks is a part of being successful—the important thing is to maintain faith in the individual's underlying ability.

Spearhead initiatives with senior leaders in your organization to support new models of working. For example, an initiative called "Men4Change" in our firm is designed to close a gender gap in senior leadership roles. Senior men help to create and assist with customized work arrangements for many high-potential women. A "Boost" program assigns sponsors to support individuals with everything from designing their flexible work arrangements before parental leave to ensuring these agreed-on plans are successfully implemented afterward.

We have not only a moral imperative to make it possible for more people to return to work from parental leave but also a commercial imperative to develop the best-performing teams. As you navigate your own return, take time to step back and figure out what you really want to accomplish. Find the sponsors who can help you shape and accelerate your career on your own terms. Then pay it forward by being an effective role model and sponsor to other new parents coming up through the ranks after you.

Adapted from content posted on hbr.org, April 9, 2020 (product #H05JR3).

18

A Working Parent's Survival Guide

by Daisy Dowling

Quick Takes

- Rehearse your transitions ahead of time
- Audit your commitments
- Plan your calendar
- Frame and recast your working-parent messages
- Use "today plus 20 years" thinking
- Revisit and recast your professional identity and brand

J acob was a partner at a respected consulting firm and—to his delight—an expectant father. As the due date loomed, though, he became increasingly apprehensive. How would he and his wife, who worked long hours as a physician, find optimal childcare? Was it possible to use his firm's generous paternity leave without negative judgment from his colleagues and clients? And with his "road warrior" schedule, how could he be a present, loving father to his new daughter?

Gabriela, a venture-capital fundraiser, went to great lengths to balance the needs of sophisticated investors, her firm's partners, and her two small children. But she frequently felt overloaded and wondered if her managers looked askance at her trips to the pediatrician's office and preschool. She confessed to some nervousness about her typical 5:30 p.m. departure from the office ("I never used to leave so early"), and she worried that she wasn't being offered stretch assignments that would lead to promotion.

Connie was a senior IT manager at a consumer-products company and a single mother to a teenage son. She was having a tough time helping him navigate the complex college-admissions process while delivering against tight turnarounds at work. And each late night at the office was a stark reminder of how little time she had left with him at home. Under the strain, Connie found herself becoming snappish at work—which senior management had begun to notice.

Jacob, Gabriela, and Connie—I've changed their names and certain details about them here—are smart, hardworking professionals, deeply committed to their organizations. But they are just as committed to their children. So all three are grappling with what I call the *working-parent problem*: the enormous task, both logistical and emotional, of earning a living and building a career while being an engaged and loving mother or father.

The problem is real and pervasive, and for moms and dads coping with it day to day, it can seem overwhelming. But it doesn't have to be that way. We can all gain more calm, confidence, and control, thereby strengthening our ability to succeed at—and even enjoy—working parenthood.

In this article, we'll take a closer look at the core challenges, and then we'll cover a few effective ways to address them. We'll also see how Jacob, Gabriela, and Connie successfully put these ideas into practice—and how you can, too.

Understanding the Five Core Challenges

When facing the pressures of working parenthood, ask yourself: What kind of difficulty am I dealing with? Most likely, it's one or more of the following.

Transition

This challenge occurs when your status quo has been upended and you're scrambling to adapt. Going back to work after parental leave is the classic, visible example. But working-parent transitions occur regularly, in many different forms. The kids get out of school for the summer and their schedules shift; you hire a new sitter and have to integrate her into your family's routine; as you walk in the door after a business trip, you have to suddenly pivot from professional to caregiving mode.

Practicalities

This challenge consists of all the to-do's and logistical matters, large and small, that consume so much of your days—and nights. Searching for the right childcare, making it to the pediatrician's appointment on time (and then dashing to the pharmacy to pick up the antibiotics), getting the kids fed each evening, and taking an important conference call with a fussy toddler in the background all fall into this category.

Communication

You face this challenge when you've got working-parent matters to discuss and you find yourself at a loss for words or at risk of being misunderstood. Perhaps you are announcing a pregnancy, asking your boss for a flexible working arrangement, negotiating the day care pickup schedule with your partner, or telling your 5-year-old that you'll be traveling for work again. The stakes are high, and your intentions are good. But the honest, constructive conversation you want to have feels frustratingly out of reach.

Loss

This challenge involves a kind of mourning. Maybe the baby took her first steps while you were at work, or you weren't staffed to a career-making project because you made a deliberate decision to work fewer hours. Now you're worried that in trying to combine work and family, you've missed out on what's truly important.

Identity

You experience this challenge when grappling with the inevitable either/or thinking and personal conflict that comes with working parenthood. Will Thursday find you at your son's debate tournament or at the big sales meeting with the new client? Are you a hard-charger or a nurturing, accessible parent? Which is right, and which is *you?* You wish you had clearer answers.

Solutions—and Prevention

As every working parent knows, these challenges are never 100% resolved. They can, however, be preempted, mitigated, and managed. Five of the most powerful ways to do that are: *rehearsing* your transitions; *auditing* your commitments and *planning* your calendar; *framing* your working-parent messages; *using "today plus 20 years" thinking*; and *revisiting and recasting* your professional identity and brand. Let's explore each technique in turn.

Rehearsing

Transitions are inevitable, but they're made easier through practice. For example, if you're returning from parental leave, stage an "as if" morning a few days early: Get the baby ready, do the caregiving handover, and commute as though you're really going to work. If you're switching childcare providers, make the new sitter's first day a dry run while you work from home, available for questions. If you're coming home from a business trip or a long stint at work, take a moment while en route to plan how you'll pivot into parenting: how you'll greet the kids, how you'll spend the evening together.

Run-throughs like these reveal potential snags (drop-off takes longer than you expected; the sitter doesn't know where to find the extra diapers; you catch yourself mulling over your performance review while putting your first-grader to bed). More important, rehearsing gives you time to iron out the wrinkles. It gets you out of working-parent "improv mode" and provides a comforting sense of "I've got this; I know that what I'm doing works."

Auditing and planning

Like every busy working parent, you're doing more and have a broader range of commitments than ever before. That means that you need to become as mindful and deliberate as possible about where your time and sweat equity are going and why—or risk practical-challenge overload.

Try sitting down with your complete calendar, your to-do list(s), and a red pen. Highlight the commitments, tasks, and obligations you could have put off, handled more efficiently, delegated, automated, or said no to over the past week—and then do the same for the week ahead. If you don't *have* to be at an upcoming meeting, for example, bow out and free up the hour; if you're ordering the same household products each week, set up regular delivery. Be ruthless—and look for themes. Maybe you have a hard time declining volunteer requests from the kids' school, or you routinely run too many revisions on the quarterly budget numbers.

Practically, this exercise can create some much-needed slack in your calendar and shorten your to-do list. Emotionally, it gives you a sense of agency: You're being proactive and taking charge. And the personal insights that come out of it ("I say yes too often"; "I can be a perfectionist") help you make more-conscious judgments about your time and your commitments for the future.

Framing

To make any working-parent communication easier and more effective, think of yourself as putting it inside a frame, defined on four sides by your *priorities, next steps, commitment*, and *enthusiasm*.

Let's say it's a particularly hectic afternoon at work, but you need to duck out of the office for your daughter's ballet recital. Tell colleagues, "I'm leaving now for my daughter's recital, but I'll be back at 3:30. I'll tackle the marketing summary then, so we have a fresh version to review tomorrow. I'm looking forward to getting this in front of the client!" A statement like that will work much better than a sheepish "I'm headed out for a few hours," because it brings listeners into your full professional and personal plan, allays any concerns about progress on pressing work, and showcases your dedication to the team. You've taken control of your own narrative and kept it positive and authentic, while minimizing the chance of misunderstandings.

Using "today plus 20 years" thinking

As a professional, you probably have incentives to focus on the intermediate term: You're rewarded for completing that six-month project, meeting your annual revenue targets, and delivering a compelling three-year strategy plan. But as a working mother or father, that time horizon is emotionally treacherous; it's where much of the working-parent downside sits and where the potential sense of loss looms largest. If you're just back from parental leave, for example, sitting miserably at your desk and missing the baby, it can be crushing to think forward six months or a year.

So try this instead when you're feeling conflicted or confronting the loss challenge: Think very short term and very long term—at the same time. Yes, you do miss the baby terribly right now, but you'll be home to see her in a few hours—and years from now you know you'll have provided her with a superb example of tenacity, career commitment, and hard work. In other words, acknowledge the reality and depth of your current feelings, identify a point of imminent relief, and then project far forward to ultimate, positive outcomes.

Revisiting and recasting

Most of us have deeply ingrained views of who we are as professionals and how we wish to be known. But it's important to revisit and update the details of those identities and brands after becoming parents. If responsiveness has always been a key part of your identity, for example, now during family dinner you're likely to feel torn: irresponsible if you ignore your smartphone and guilt-ridden as a parent if you check it. What used to be a positive career differentiator has become a classic no-win situation, and you've lost both pride in your professional self and the happy moment of being an engaged mom or dad eating with the kids.

To be clear, recasting doesn't mean lowering your standards; it means defining important new ones. To help in the process, try completing the following sentences: "I am a working-parent professional who . . ."; "I prioritize work responsibilities when . . ."; and "My kids come before work when. . . ." Through this exercise, you may decide that instead of putting so much weight on being responsive, you choose to think of yourself as an efficient, thoughtful, or articulate communicator—and you may vow that barring a work emergency, your kids take precedence during dinner.

Putting It All Together

Remember Jacob, the expectant father? Like most working parents, he was feeling the pressures of multiple core challenges, and he wanted to contain their impact on his upcoming parental leave and eventual return to work. He began by *framing* his conversations with clients: announcing his impending absence, previewing his time out of the office, reiterating his dedication, and describing how his team would see critical advisory projects through. To Jacob's surprise, the message was warmly received; it even allowed him to deepen and personalize several relationships that had previously been all-business. Next, after carefully *auditing* his post-leave calendar, Jacob determined that a number of his work meetings in faraway cities could be done remotely, freeing up additional precious time to spend with his little girl. (Later, when he *was* on the road, he reminded himself that the trip was short and the return home would be joyous—and that his career success would help ensure a stable financial future for the entire family.) During his month at home, he and his wife also anticipated and *rehearsed* their caregiving plans, deciding that they would ask for supplemental help from family members on the days she was on call. Several months into working fatherhood, Jacob reported being busier than ever but feeling in charge and on track.

As for Gabriela, she concluded that in trying to be all things to all people, she had taken on too much. *Recasting* her identity as "future partner in the firm and devoted mom" helped her identify commitments that didn't align with either role. She kept all her investor responsibilities, continued leaving the office at the same time, and went to the pediatrician's when needed. But she quietly began cutting back on internal work—such as organizing the firm's annual retreat—and she limited her volunteerism at the kids' school to one event per semester. The professional recasting process also gave her the time, clarity, and confidence to prepare for effective conversations with her managers, in which she better *framed* her ambitions and desired schedule.

Connie realized that the combination of job pressures and her son's impending departure for college had created new challenges in her working-parent life. Together, we came up with a plan to mitigate the effects on her personally and professionally. After *auditing* her calendar and her to-do's, she delegated several recurring tasks to more-junior members of her team and dedicated the hours saved to a weekly evening outing with her son. When college-application and work deadlines collided, she used *framing* techniques to calmly explain her time out of the office to her colleagues instead of snapping at them, and she used the *"today plus 20 years"* tool to put her situation into perspective. Additionally, when her son was away visiting colleges, Connie *rehearsed* her evenings and weekends as an empty nester. With new habits in place, her stress subsided.

Conclusion

Working parenthood isn't easy. It's a big, complex, emotional, chronic, and sometimes all-consuming struggle. But as with any challenge, the more you break it down, the less daunting it becomes. With a clearer view of the issues you're facing, and with specific strategies for managing them, you'll be better able to succeed at work—and be the mother or father you want to be at home.

Adapted from an article in Harvard Business Review, *July–August 2019 (product #R1904L).*

Epilogue

Find *Your* Success

"The One Thing I Wish I Had Known . . ."

Contributed by 18 HBR readers

Quick Takes

- Ask confidently for the support you need at work
- Returning to work brings guilt and emotional toll for many
- Others will find returning from leave invigorating
- The long view is hard to see at first, but you will get there
- Don't try to be the person you were before you were a parent

Editors' Note: We asked HBR readers on Instagram a simple question: **What's the one thing you wish you had known when you returned to work as a first-time parent?** Insightful and inspiring comments came in by the dozens, and we're sharing a handful of them here.

I wish I understood the power of the "ask." I assumed my employer would say no if I requested more flexibility or alternative working arrangements. Looking back on it, I should have felt confident in asking. Most employers will likely want to work with you to make life a little easier and retain great talent. Don't just assume the answer is no! You may be surprised with the outcome if you just ask the question.

   —startinggate_peopleops

I wish I had known better to set boundaries between work and home; and that giving 80% at work and 80% at home is more than enough most of the time, rather than trying to give 150% at both.

   —stephanie_de_sm

We might get little flexibility at work, but we have to perform more/extra than before just to prove for every task that we are not taking advantage of the flexibility and are the same efficient person as before!
—pravaradeshpande

That the expectation of both society and myself to be able to come back ready to focus at 8 or 12 weeks postpartum is utterly ridiculous physically, mentally, and emotionally and is in direct opposition to what science and experts in these fields tell us.
—aameador1

The guilt. Because it can be hard to perform at the same level you were at before the leave. Especially on few hours of sleep and hormones. Then while trying to squeeze in nursing at work in between breaks. It's a huge emotional toll.
—legendary_wealthbuilders

Have the courage to tell your coworkers and bosses what you've been struggling with. Whether it's lack of sleep, breastfeeding and supply, and/or mom guilt for being away from your baby. If you work with the right people, they will support you and help in any way they can. If you see that there's opportunity for your organization to grow when it comes to policy or benefits for new parents, voice your opinions to HR. You could be the one that changes everything for you and future new parents.

—heatherseriously

Don't try to catch up on emails. Inbox zero. Use it as a moment to start fresh. People will tell you what you need to know.

—mariecastelli

That I would be happy to go back. I really valued being able to use my brain and focus on problem-solving. I love my daughter more than anything, but I really love my work too. Being patient with learning to balance work and mom-life takes time—be gentle on yourself.

—msbcooke

It's OK if you don't miss your baby. I was one of those moms who was relieved to go back to work. I felt so incompetent at home as a new mom, and work gave me some sense of competence. I felt horribly guilty for not missing him during the day. I rushed like hell to get home and see him at the end of the day though!

—amandachoudhary

Kids get sick a lot, and you will also get sick a lot more than you used to. There is no easy answer. Just go into it having the right expectation and be kind to yourself.

—legerejason

While I labored (no pun intended) over detailed hand-over documents prior to going out on maternity leave, I should have asked that the same be provided for me upon my return. What has changed? Who has joined? Who left? What are the most pressing issues to address first? What new tools are we using and how can I go about learning them?

—vg_murray

That I shouldn't be apologetic about being a mother. Before kids, I was very careful about keeping my private life separate from my work life. Now I have made it clear that while I value my job, my kids come first, and if I need time off to tend to that, I let my team know.

—lindajean2020

I wish I could see the long view. I was jealous and sad that my awesome sitter got to spend so much time with my baby. But then at 3, he went to preschool with a new teacher. Then kindergarten and school with new teachers and coaches and other adults. Now he's almost 19 and I see that it's his parents who have been the constants in his life. It's so hard to take the long view when you have an infant.

—jkessbrown

That a happy family is better than a clean house.

—whiskeyterrierfoxtrot

You'll be surprised by how much better at time management you become. You won't be able to work those same long hours, but you will find that by setting work hour boundaries you're actually more efficient and productive. I was very surprised by this realization after my first baby and it has made me a better employee and manager.

—katekatherinekat

Your child won't love you any less when you come back through that door eight hours later.

—ls.loo

I wish I knew from the beginning how important it is to have honest conversations with your manager and co-workers about expectations and support needed, everyday logistical challenges, and mental health. Opening the door to talk about these difficult and personal topics clearly set the foundation of a good work environment and finding solutions together.

—yasminlenz_

You have gone through a life-changing experience and you will not be the person you were before. Do not chase that person. Define who you are now as a working parent and still show up and be great.

—raisingblackboyjoy

NOTES

Chapter 2

1. Loes Meeussen and Colette Van Laar, "Feeling Pressure to Be a Perfect Mother Relates to Parental Burnout and Career Ambitions," *Frontiers in Psychology* 9, no. 2113 (2013).

2. Catherine Caruso, "Pregnancy Causes Lasting Changes in a Woman's Brain," *Scientific American*, December 19, 2016, https:// www.scientificamerican.com/article/pregnancy-causes-lasting -changes-in-a-womans-brain/.

Chapter 3

1. Bureau of Labor Statistics, "Employment Characteristics of Families—2019," news release, April 21, 2020, https://www.bls.gov/ news.release/pdf/famee.pdf.

2. Liana S. Leach et al., "Prevalence and Course of Anxiety Disorders (and Symptom Levels) in Men Across the Perinatal Period," *Journal of Affective Disorders* 190 (2016): 675–686, https://pubmed .ncbi.nlm.nih.gov/26590515/#affiliation-1.

3. Cleber José Aló de Moraes and Tania Mara Marques Granato, "Becoming a Father: An Integrative Review of the Literature on Transition to Fatherhood," *Psicologia em Estudo* 21, no. 4 (2017): 557–567, https://www.researchgate.net/publication/315762206 _BECOMING_A_FATHER_AN_INTEGRATIVE_REVIEW_OF _THE_LITERATURE_ON_TRANSITION_TO_FATHERHOOD.

4. Bianca Wordley, "The Men Who Find the Transition to Fatherhood Most Difficult," *Essential Baby*, March 16, 2018, http://www .essentialbaby.com.au/pregnancy/news-views/the-men-who-find -the-transition-to-fatherhood-most-difficult-20180315-h0xjs2.

5. Aló de Moraes and Marques Granato, "Becoming a Father."

6. Samantha J. Teague and Adrian B. R. Shatte, "Exploring the Transition to Fatherhood," *JMIR Pediatrics and Parenting* 1, no. 2 (2018), https://www.ncbi.nlm.nih.gov/pmc/articles/PMC6715057/.

7. Brad Harrington and Jamie Ladge, "The New Dad: Exploring Fatherhood Within a Career Context," Boston College, June 2010, https://www.researchgate.net/publication/259266390_The_New_Dad_Exploring_Fatherhood_within_a_Career_Context_Boston_College.

8. Harrington and Ladge, "The New Dad."

Chapter 4

1. Preeti Varathan, "Modern Parents Spend More Time with Their Kids Than Their Parents Spent with Them," Quartz, November 30, 2017, https://qz.com/1143092/study-modern-parents-spend-more-time-with-their-kids-than-their-parents-spent-with-them/.

2. Gretchen Livingston and Kim Parker, "8 Facts About American Dads," FactTank, Pew Research Center, June 12, 2019, https://www.pewresearch.org/fact-tank/2019/06/12/fathers-day-facts/.

3. Gretchen Livingston, "Growing Number of Dads Home with Kids," Pew Research Center, June 5, 2014, https://www.pewsocialtrends.org/2014/06/05/growing-number-of-dads-home-with-the-kids/.

4. Kathryn Vasel, "It Costs $233,610 to Raise a Child," CNN Money, January 9, 2017, https://money.cnn.com/2017/01/09/pf/cost-of-raising-a-child-2015/index.html; Care.com editorial staff, "Child Care Costs More in 2020, and the Pandemic Has Parents Scrambling for Solutions," Care.com, June 15, 2020, https://www.care.com/c/stories/2423/how-much-does-child-care-cost/.

5. Wendy Klein, Carolina Izquierdo, and Thomas N. Bradbury, "The Difference Between a Happy Marriage and a Miserable One: Chores," *Atlantic*, March 1, 2013, https://www.theatlantic.com/

sexes/archive/2013/03/the-difference-between-a-happy-marriage -and-miserable-one-chores/273615/.

Chapter 5

1. Sara Raley, Suzanne M. Bianchi, and Wendy Wang, "When Do Fathers Care? Mothers' Economic Contribution and Fathers' Involvement in Child Care," *PMC* 117, no. 5 (2012): 1422–1459, https://www.ncbi.nlm.nih.gov/pmc/articles/PMC4568757/#!po=8 .13953.

2. Shelley Correll, Stephan Benard, and In Paik, "Mothers Face Penalties in Hiring, Starting Salaries, and Perceived Competence While Fathers Can Benefit from Being a Parent," *American Journal of Sociology* 112, no. 5 (March 2007): 1297–1339, https://gap .hks.harvard.edu/getting-job-there-motherhood-penalty.

3. Amanda Barroso and Juliana Menasce Horowitz, *The Pandemic Has Highlighted Many Challenges for Mothers, but They Aren't Necessarily New* (Washington, DC: Pew Research Center, March 17, 2021, https://www.pewresearch.org/fact-tank/2021 /03/17/the-pandemic-has-highlighted-many-challenges-for -mothers-but-they-arent-necessarily-new/#:~:text=and%20family %20responsibilities.-,Work%20and%20family,work%20hours%20 (54%25%20vs.

4. Jill E. Yavorsky, Claire M. Kamp Dush, and Sarah K. Schoppe-Sullivan, "The Production of Inequality: The Gender Division of Labor Across the Transition to Parenthood," *Journal of Marriage and Family* 77, no. 2 (June 2015): 662–679.

5. Ashley V. Whillans, Jessie Pow, and Michael I. Norton, "Buying Time Promotes Relationship Satisfaction," working paper 18-072, Harvard Business School, Boston, January 2018 (revised January 2020), https://www.hbs.edu/faculty/Pages/item.aspx? num=53939.

6. According to Stephen Jenkins, a professor at the London School of Economics, cited in Amelia Hill, "Men Become Richer After

Divorce," *The Guardian*, January 24, 2009, https://www.theguard
ian.com/lifeandstyle/2009/jan/25/divorce-women-research.

Chapter 8

1. "Home Sharing," CoAbode, https://www.coabode.org
/programs/program/1.

2. Skye Schooley, "What Is Flextime, and Why Should You Offer
It?," business.com, November 12, 2020, https://www.business.com
/articles/advantages-of-flextime/.

3. Jennifer Wolf, "The Positive Effects of Single Parenting
on Kids," Verywell Family, November 13, 2019, https://www
.verywellfamily.com/positive-effects-of-single-parenting-2997390.

Chapter 10

1. Kim Parker, *Working-Mom Guilt? Many Dads Feel It Too*
(Washington, DC: Pew Research Center, April 1, 2015), https://
www.pewresearch.org/fact-tank/2015/04/01/working-mom-guilt
-many-dads-feel-it-too/.

2. Gretchen Livingston, *They're Waiting Longer, but U.S. Women
Today More Likely to Have Children Than a Decade Ago* (Washington, DC: Pew Research Center, January 18, 2018), https://www
.pewresearch.org/social-trends/2018/01/18/theyre-waiting-longer
-but-u-s-women-today-more-likely-to-have-children-than-a
-decade-ago/.

3. Kaamini Chanrai, "If Men Want a Greater Caring Role (and They
Do!), What's Stopping Them?," My Family Care, November 27, 2018,
https://www.myfamilycare.co.uk/resources/news/men-want-greater
-caring-role-what-is-stopping-them?utm_source=Sign-Up.to.

Chapter 11

1. Hannah Riley Bowles, Bobbi J. Thomason, and Julia B. Bear,
"Reconceptualizing What and How Women Negotiate for Career

Advancement " *Academy of Management Journal* 62, no. 6 (2019), https:// doi.org/10.5465/amj.2017.1497.

Chapter 14

1. William J. Strawbridge, Sarah J. Schema, and Robert E. Roberts, "Impact of Spouses' Sleep Problems on Partners," *Sleep* 27, no. 3 (May 2004): 527–531; Amie M. Gordon and Serena Chen, "The Role of Sleep in Interpersonal Conflict: Do Sleepless Nights Mean Worse Fights?," *Social Psychology and Personality Science* 5, no. 2 (2014): 168–175; Angela M. Hicks and Lisa M. Diamond, "Don't Go to Bed Angry: Attachment, Conflict, and Affective and Physiological Reactivity," *Personal Relationships* 18, no. 2 (2011): 266–284.

2. Mona El-Sheikh et al., "Marital Conflict and Disruption of Children's Sleep," *Child Development* 77, no. 1 (2006): 31–43; Chrystyna D. Kouros and Mona El-Sheikh, "Within-Family Relations in Objective Sleep Duration, Quality, and Schedule," *Child Development* 6, no. 6 (2007): 1983–2000; Annie Bernier et al., "Mothers, Fathers, and Toddlers: Parental Psychosocial Functioning as a Context for Young Children's Sleep," *Developmental Psychology* 49, no. 7 (2013): 1375–1384.

3. Lucy S. King et al., "Mothers' Postpartum Sleep Disturbance Is Associated with the Ability to Sustain Sensitivity Toward Infants," *Sleep Medicine* 65 (2010): 74–83; Teresa A. Lillis et al., "Sleep Quality Buffers the Effects of Negative Social Interactions on Maternal Mood in the 3–6 Month Postpartum Period: A Daily Diary Study," *Journal of Behavioral Medicine* 41 (2018): 733–746.

4. Christopher M. Barnes, "Research: Your Abusive Boss Is Probably an Insomniac," *Harvard Business Review*, November 2014; Cristiano Guarana and Christopher M. Barnes, "Research: Sleep Deprivation Can Make It Harder to Stay Calm at Work," *Harvard Business Review*, August 2017; Christopher M. Barnes, "Research: Sleep-Deprived Leaders Are Less Inspiring," *Harvard Business Review*, June 2016; Christopher M. Barnes and Nathaniel F. Watson,

"Why Healthy Sleep Is Good for Business," *Sleep Medicine Reviews* 47 (2019): 112–118.

Chapter 15

1. "Postpartum Depression," Mayo Clinic, https://www.mayo clinic.org/diseases-conditions/postpartum-depression/symptoms -causes/syc-20376617.

Chapter 17

1. Susan Harkness, Magda Borkowska, and Alina Pelikh, "Employment Pathways and Occupational Change After Childbirth," Government Equalities Office, October 2019, https://assets .publishing.service.gov.uk/government/uploads/system/uploads/ attachment_data/file/840062/Bristol_Final_Report_1610.pdf.

2. Claudia Goldin, "A Grand Gender Convergence: Its Last Chapter," *American Economic Review* 104, no. 4 (2014): 1091–1119.

ABOUT THE CONTRIBUTORS

DAISY DOWLING, SERIES EDITOR, is the founder and CEO of Workparent, the executive coaching and training firm, and author of *Workparent: The Complete Guide to Succeeding on the Job, Staying True to Yourself, and Raising Happy Kids* (Harvard Business Review Press, 2021). She is a full-time working parent to two young children. She can be reached at www.workparent.com.

CHRISTOPHER M. BARNES is a professor of organizational behavior at the University of Washington's Foster School of Business. He worked in the Fatigue Countermeasures branch of the Air Force Research Laboratory before pursuing his PhD in organizational behavior at Michigan State University and has kept sleep as his primary research interest. He has twin infants and a preschooler and thus understands sleep deprivation from an experiential perspective as well.

JULIA BECK is the founder of the It's Working Project and Forty Weeks. Ms. Beck, a passionate strategist, storyteller, ideator, and connector, is based in Washington, DC, where she is the matriarch of a blended family that includes a loving husband, a loyal golden retriever, and four children—all of whom are her favorite. Find her @TheJuliaBeck.

CHRISTINE MICHEL CARTER is a subject matter expert on working parents and women's ERGs. She speaks frequently at conferences and corporate events on subjects such as maternal mental health, retaining women of color, and combating impostor syndrome. As a *ForbesWomen* senior contributor, she has written hundreds of articles aimed at helping and advocating for working parents. Christine has interviewed Vice President Kamala Harris on Black maternal health and has received congressional citation for her work in ensuring moms of color have access to vital information. And on top of raising her two school-age kids, she's the author of the novel *MOM AF* and the children's book *Can Mommy Go to Work?*

COURTNEY CASHMAN is a senior associate editor at Harvard Business Review Press. When she's not working, she often takes on the roles of baker, crafter, dance partner, song writer, and couch for her two wonderful kids.

JACKIE COLEMAN is a former marriage counselor and most recently worked on education programs for the state of Georgia.

JOHN COLEMAN is a coauthor of the book *Passion and Purpose: Stories from the Best and Brightest Young Busi-*

ness Leaders. Follow him on Twitter @johnwcoleman. Jackie and John have four sweet, mischievous kids ranging from newborn to seven years old, who keep life crazy, full, and fulfilling.

CARRIE CRONKEY is chief marketing officer of Care.com.

KEVIN EVERS is a senior editor at Harvard Business Review Press.

BRUCE FEILER is the author of seven *New York Times* bestsellers, including *Council of Dads,* which inspired the NBC television series, and *The Secrets of Happy Families.* His two TED Talks have been viewed more than 2 million times. His latest book is *Life Is in the Transitions: Mastering Change at Any Age.* He lives in Brooklyn with his wife, Linda Rottenberg, and their identical twin daughters Eden and Tybee. For more information, please visit brucefeiler.com.

AMIE M. GORDON is an assistant professor of psychology at the University of Michigan, Ann Arbor, where she directs the Well-Being, Health, and Interpersonal Relationships Lab (WHIRL). She received her PhD in social-personality psychology from the University of California, Berkeley. As a working mother who functions best on nine hours of sleep, much of her research on sleep and its effects on relationships has been inspired by her own nights of sleep deprivation.

REBECCA KNIGHT is currently a senior correspondent at *Insider,* covering careers and the workplace. Previously she was a freelance journalist and a lecturer at Wesleyan University. Her work has been published in the *New York Times, USA Today,* and the *Financial Times.* She is the mom of two tweenage daughters.

JANNA KORETZ is a psychologist and the founder of Azimuth, which provides therapy focused on the unique challenges of individuals in high-pressure careers. As the mother of a 1-year-old, Janna spends a lot of time each day getting her webcam angle just right so that the growing mess behind her camera cannot be seen by her colleagues.

CAROL T. KULIK is a research professor of human resource management at the University of South Australia Business School. Her research investigates how employees can negotiate employment arrangements that benefit both parties in the employment relationship, with a particular interest in customized work arrangements that enable women and mature-age people to thrive. She believes that one-size-fits-all work arrangements prevent organizations from leveraging the value of employee diversity.

MARIKA LINDHOLM founded ESME.com to ignite a social movement of solo moms. A trained sociologist, Marika taught courses on inequality, diversity, and gender at Northwestern University for over a decade. Marika is also the coeditor of the award-winning anthology *We Got This: Solo Mom Stories of Grit, Heart, and Humor*, which celebrates solo mothers' tenacity, courage, and fierce love for their children.

LISA QUEST is the London-based head of Oliver Wyman's Public Policy practice in the United Kingdom and Ireland. With two young boys, she divides her time between reading *Thomas the Tank Engine*, building forts, and drinking way too much coffee.

EVE RODSKY is a lawyer and the founder of the Philanthropy Advisory Group, which advises high-net-worth families and charitable foundations on best practices for harmonious operations, governance, and disposition of funds. She is the author of *Fair Play: A Game-Changing Solution for When You Have Too Much to Do (and More Life to Live)*. Eve and her husband Seth are raising their two sons and daughter to be gender justice advocates who pride themselves on knowing that taking out the garbage isn't complete until a fresh bag goes back in the bin.

RUCHI SINHA is a senior lecturer (assistant professor) of management at the University of South Australia

Business School. Her PhD is in organizational psychology, and her research explores how employees negotiate at work, especially expressing voice and managing power/status conflicts with leaders and within teams. Ruchi has spent long periods as a solo parent while her partner worked in a different city and has learned to create a village of friends and negotiate flexibility with her employer and her preteen daughter.

AMY JEN SU is a cofounder and managing partner of Paravis Partners, a premier executive coaching and leadership development firm. For the past two decades, she has coached CEOs, executives, and rising stars in organizations. She is the author of *The Leader You Want to Be* (Harvard Business Review Press, 2019) and a coauthor of *Own the Room* (Harvard Business Review Press, 2013) with Muriel Maignan Wilkins. Amy is also a full-time working parent with a teenage son who is currently in high school.

AVIVAH WITTENBERG-COX is the CEO of 20-first, one of the world's leading gender consulting firms, and author of *Seven Steps to Leading a Gender-Balanced Business*.

INDEX

Find fulfillment at home and at work with the HBR Working Parents Series

Advice for Working Dads

Advice for Working Moms

Communicate Better with Everyone

Getting It All Done

Managing Your Career

Taking Care of Yourself

FOR MORE, VISIT **HBR.ORG/BOOKS**

Harvard Business Review Press